AUGUST
RECKONING

AUGUST RECKONING

Jack Turner and Racism in
Post-Civil War Alabama

WILLIAM WARREN ROGERS
and
ROBERT DAVID WARD

LOUISIANA STATE UNIVERSITY PRESS · BATON ROUGE

To Hazel Richards
and Elizabeth Ireland Poe
and to Jane

ISBN 0-8071-0209-1
Library of Congress Catalog Card Number 72-96401
Copyright © 1973 by Louisiana State University Press
All rights reserved
Manufactured in the United States of America
Printed by Vail-Ballou Press, Inc., Binghamton, New York
Designed by Albert Crochet

Contents

Acknowledgments

A NUMBER OF INDIVIDUALS and institutions greatly aided the authors in writing this book. We wish to extend appreciation to the library and archival staffs of Auburn University, the University of Alabama, the University of North Carolina, Florida State University, the Mobile Public Library, the New Orleans Public Library, the Choctaw County Public Library, the Alabama Department of Archives and History, the Federal Records Center at East Point, Georgia, the National Archives, and the Library of Congress.

A grant from the National Endowment for the Humanities made possible the time for travel, research, and writing.

While totally absolving them from any responsibility for the book's contents, we would like to thank the following persons for their advice and encouragement: John H. Moore, Carlisle Floyd, Terence H. Nolan, Irving Fleet, Jerrell H. Shofner, Maurice Vance, Milo B. Howard, Allen W. Jones, the late Jack E. Kendrick, Robert B. Ingram, Donald Smith, Stonewall B. Stickney, John S. Neel, Wilbur E. Dearman, Mrs. Wayne (Lanelle) Turner, the Reverend George Myers, Mrs. Clara Turner, Mrs. Arthur C. (Mattie Jo) Glover, the Reverend Harry E. Rogers, Mrs. Charley Turner, Mrs. Ann H. Gay (who was helpful beyond "the call of duty"), William H. Barber, Mrs. J. R. (Gloria) Mosley, W. B. Adams, Miss Sue Doggett, Murray Gibson, and Mrs. Marie Miller. Charles East, Leslie E. Phillabaum, and Martha L. Hall of Louisiana State University Press were at all times helpful and sympathetic. Our wives, Miriam Rogers and Jane Ward, were kind but critical, and they believed in the book.

Without doubt this book contains errors of fact. Although they were not deliberate, they were inevitable, and they are the fault of the authors.

black man. In a society where the accumulation of money bore integral relation to the possession of power, the Negro was tragically unarmed.

As for politics, the Negro was frequently discouraged from voting, but not until the Populists courted Negro votes in the 1890s and threatened Bourbon supremacy (surely Jack Turner would have been pleased that Choctaw County became a Populist bastion, the only one in the Black Belt) was there a movement for mass disfranchisement. Before that, what was important to the Bourbons was how the Negroes voted, and their votes were, as a matter of course, manipulated and controlled. After the Bourbons came to power, government and politics and all their trappings—the rewards of office, fame, the awarding of contracts, the right to draft, pass, and enforce legislation—were the domain of the white race and Negro participation was by sufferance.

Jack Turner refused to accept a society so structured. This book recounts the story of how he attempted to change his world. No collection of the black man's papers is on deposit in Alabama's state archives or in any of the state universities or at the Library of Congress. Semiliterate at best, Jack left few written records other than his signature. Because of this, the authors have not used the traditional biographical form. Certain events in his life can never be known because there simply is no record of them. But contemporary newspapers, state and federal documents, numerous county records, and the letters and writings of people with whom he had contact (or who were in some way affected by his life) have been consulted and used.

Jack's role as a political figure within the black community and the Republican party was an important aspect of his life. Material covering this phase is incomplete, but fortunately, major events and conditions can be documented. Far more satisfactory are the diverse and revealing sources that concern the most important aspect of Turner: his role as a symbol. In truth, he symbolized one thing to a majority of his white neighbors—an uppity black. To a minority of whites he was an evil symbol, nothing less than a threat to their way of life. But to the blacks Jack Turner was a symbol of courage and strength.

Although no biography can ever be "total," this study is, in the orthodox sense, more imperfect than most. The attempt has been to render a microcosmic illumination of the development of politics in Alabama and the South in the decades after the Civil War. Further, the life and death of Jack Turner offer insight into the tragedy of race relations during this period.

Preface

JACK TURNER was a black man who lived in Choctaw
County, a part of Alabama's famous Black Belt—a tier
of counties stretching across the south-central part of the
state and noted for its dark, productive soil and heavy
concentration of Negroes. Yet the truth is that geographi-
cally and in other ways, Choctaw County could not decide whether it was in the Black Belt or not, an ambivalent condition that had important effects on the life of
Jack Turner. Born a slave about 1840, he won his
freedom when the Civil War ended and within the next
few years emerged as a leader of his race. But with the
end of Radical Reconstruction in 1874, an emerged and
emerging set of conditions confronted the black leader
and seemed to make his bid for equality and dignity
hopeless.

The decades of Bourbon ascendancy came after 1874,
as Alabama became a state whose institutions were
frankly, admittedly, unashamedly, and triumphantly
dominated by whites. The theory of white supremacy and
black inferiority found daily expression and constant ap-
plication. If Caucasian dominance became legally fixed

and formalized (as it did), Anglo-Saxon superiority was
no less manifest in unstated ways. If a white man and a
black man met face to face on a narrow walk, it was the
black who stepped aside to let the other pass; a white
man's surname was always prefaced with "Mister," or
some sort of title, a Negro's never; purchases paid for in
cash primarily involved the color green until a merchant
was confronted simultaneously with two customers whom
he must accommodate according to black or white.

White superiority was no less evident in a verbal folk-
lore spawned by, repeated by, and believed by whites:
Negro men were naturally lazy and without ambition,
desirous of having sexual relations with white women,
incapable of higher reasoning, uncontrollable when under the influence of liquor, and cursed forever with an
offensive body smell. And yet with all his negative qualities, the black, according to the Southern mystique, given
proper guidance by his white mentors was carefree, musi-
cal, naïve, gentle, mercurial, anatomically limber, religious (in an outlandish way), and humorous. Still, the
black race, as everyone knew, *was* inferior, and all things
proceeded from this basic premise.

Schools at all levels were separate and unequal. With
a few exceptions white people worshipped in white
churches and heard sermons by white preachers, while
black congregations gathered in black churches and
listened to the discourses of black ministers. Presumably
both races prayed to the same God and were somehow
hopeful of the same hereafter—but in the here and now
religious life was firmly segregated. The Negro did not
achieve economic independence. In the debased, sub-
marginal world of tenant farmers and sharecroppers, the
unenvied place on the bottom rail was occupied by the

AUGUST
RECKONING

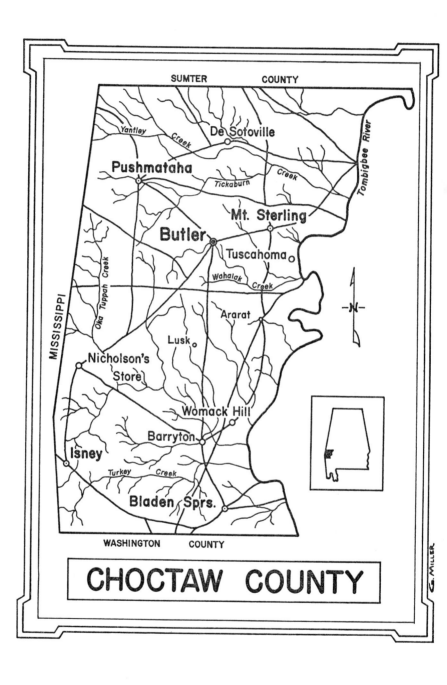

SUMTER COUNTY

Yantley Creek

De Sotoville

Pushmataha

Tickaburn Creek

Tombigbee River

Mt. Sterling

Butler

Tuscahoma

Oka Tuppah Creek

Wahalak Creek

MISSISSIPPI

Ararat

Lusk

Nicholson's
Store

Womack Hill

Barryton

Isney

Turkey Creek

Bladen Sprs.

WASHINGTON COUNTY

CHOCTAW COUNTY

G. MILLER

1

The Setting

CHOCTAW COUNTY, the stage for Jack Turner's turbulent life and political martyrdom, was created by an act of the General Assembly of Alabama in December, 1847. Located in the southwestern part of the state, the new entity contained 916 square miles—some 553,776 acres of undulating land—and was carved out of the older counties of Sumter to the north and Washington to the south. The western boundary was the Mississippi state line, and on the east the broad Tombigbee River formed a languid, winding demarcation separating Choctaw from Marengo and Clarke counties.[1]

Before the agitation for a new county, before the plows bit into the rich black soil, turning the land for cotton, and before the towns of Mount Sterling, Butler, Bladon Springs, and Tuscahoma were founded, the land belonged to the Choctaw Indians.

Deer, bears, foxes, squirrels, raccoons, and other fur-bearing animals furnished the Choctaws with food and

1. *Acts of the General Assembly of Alabama,* 1847–48, pp. 306–309, hereinafter cited as *Acts.* See also Saffold Berney, *Hand-Book of Alabama* (Birmingham, 1892), 277–78.

skins. Wild turkeys and game birds were plentiful in the seemingly endless forests of longleaf yellow pines that were interspersed with hardwoods, especially hickories, gums, and a variety of oaks. The long-haired Choctaws fished in the Tombigbee and in the numerous creeks and streams which were lined with tall switch cane. They were also excellent agriculturalists. William Woodward, who would become the first state senator from the new county, insisted that civilization could not be held back; yet Choctaw did not become civilized and settled as those terms would apply to the neighboring Black Belt counties where large cotton plantations were the rule. Choctaw County had the raw, unsettled edge of the frontier that tempered the sophisticated and aristocratic character-istics of the Black Belt.

The Choctaw Indians fought foreign invaders begin-ning with DeSoto in 1540, and after the conquistadors the French and then the English. The Choctaws estab-lished an important village at what became Mount Ster-ling, and the settlement doubled as a significant line of defense for the tribe against the Creek Indians. Only four miles away, at Red Bluff, the Choctaws maintained a major crossing point on the Tombigbee River. Later Red Bluff became known as Tuscahoma or Tuschoma Landing, developing into a convenient post for trade be-tween whites and Indians and still later a place for river steamers to pick up and land passengers and cargo.[2]

Most of what became Alabama was ceded by Great Britain to the United States in 1783, and Spain's claim to the area above the 31st parallel was relinquished in

2. Euba Eugenia DuBose, "The History of Mount Sterling," *Alabama Historical Quarterly,* XXV (Fall and Winter, 1963), 297–369. See also Frances Ford, "A History of Butler, Alabama" (Type-script in Choctaw County Public Library, Butler).

1795. The final acquisition of land—the Mobile area
—came in 1813. Alabama became a territory in 1817
and a state in 1819. The Choctaws surrendered their
lands in southwestern Alabama, including what would
become Choctaw County, by five treaties, beginning in
1805 and culminating in the notorious Treaty of Danc-
ing Rabbit Creek in 1830.[3] Eager settlers moved in to
open up new cotton lands.

When the people who founded Tuscahoma became
sick with chills and fever because of the settlement's location near the river, many of them moved four miles in-
land and established Mount Sterling. One of the early
residents was S. E. Catterlin, an able businessman who
bought horses and mules in Mount Sterling, Kentucky,
and he suggested the new communty's name. Six miles
west of Mount Sterling another hamlet grew up around
Hendrix' Crossroads (named for a pioneer settler, James
Hendrix). The community grew, and in the 1840s its
name was changed to Butler in honor of Pierce M. Butler
of South Carolina. Down the Tombigbee, Bladon Springs
soon developed into a noted watering place. Wealthy
people from Mobile and New Orleans congregated at the
spa to drink its medicinal mineral waters, and for years
Bladon Springs had the only hotel in the county. Across
the region other settlements and communities—such as
Pushmataha, named for the great Choctaw chief—sprang
up.[4]

3. See Arthur H. De Rosier, *The Removal of the Choctaw
Indians* (Knoxville, 1970), 29, 116–18; Thomas Perkins Abernethy,
The Formative Period in Alabama, 1815–1828 (University, Ala.,
1965), 48, 67.
4. DuBose, "History of Mount Sterling," 301–12; Mary B. Le
Noir, "Sketch of Butler" (Works Progress Administration [WPA]
MSS in Alabama Department of Archives and History, Mont-
gomery).

The act creating Choctaw decreed that the county seat would be located within four miles of the county's geographical center and would be known as Butler. At least 160 acres were to be set aside for a courthouse and other public buldings. While the construction was in progress, court was held at the settlement of Barryton. Two supplementary acts in January and March, 1848, required the seat of government to be within six miles of the county's center: if necessary a mathematician might be employed to fix the site. An election was set for April whereby the voters would select one of three communities as the seat of government.[5] The two other rivals were Tuscahoma and Mount Sterling—the latter town's citizens, confident of victory, had left land vacant for the public buildings. At the time, Mount Sterling was a sprawling, growing village, and Butler and Tuscahoma were slightly smaller. In any case, Butler was selected, and the courthouse was completed in 1848. Jim Hendrix donated land for a Methodist church (the building was used by all denominations for a number of years), and the village prospered. Yet Butler never won unanimous favor, and as late as 1860 there was an unsuccessful attempt to move the county seat elsewhere.[6]

By 1860 Alabama had fifty-two counties, and Choctaw ranked thirty-fourth in population, having 6,767 whites and 7,094 blacks or a total of 13,877 citizens. An unusually large number, 460, were free persons of color, a fact that might account in part for the early and active role Choctaw blacks would play in Reconstruction politics. Since the county ranked only twenty-fourth in

5. *Acts*, 1847–48, pp. 306–309, 309–10, 312.
6. *Ibid.*, 1859–60, pp. 503–506. See also information supplied by Mrs. Heyward Taylor of Butler (WPA MSS in Alabama Department of Archives and History, Montgomery).

the number of slaves, it was not a typical Black Belt domain.[7] Further evidence of Choctaw's peripheral status was in the number of slaves and slaveowners. In all there were 640 masters, 100 of whom owned 1 slave. The next to highest group was made up of 92 planters who had between 10 and 15 slaves. Only 4 citizens owned from 100 to 200 slaves and none more than that.[8]

Even by the standards of the first half of the nineteenth century, Choctaw County was cut off from the rest of the state. Rude trails sliced unevenly through the wilderness, and roads, despite a law containing strict (but apparently unenforced) requirements for work on them by the citizens, were few and far between. There was no railroad before the first Alabama, Tennessee and Northern train steamed through in 1910, and the Tombigbee remained the major route of trade and travel. Before 1900, let alone before 1860, the county's land remained largely uncultivated. In 1860 the ratio of unimproved acreage over that of improved land was almost three to one. Only three men owned more than one thousand acres, while most farms were either twenty to fifty acres or from one hundred to five hundred acres. Yet Choctaw, like other Black Belt counties, was dependent on cotton. There was little business activity that could be described as industry except for turpentine and timber—the longleaf pines made excellent ship masts; they were hewn in octagonal shapes, tapered, and floated down the Tombigbee to the port at Mobile. Although yeomen farmers and planters produced livestock, orchard products, and such field crops as sweet potatoes, corn, rye, beans, and oats, the undisputed king was cotton.

7. *Eighth Census,* 1860, Population, I, 8.
8. *Ibid.,* Agriculture, II, 223.

The county's populace paid homage to the sovereign, and in 1860 Choctaw County ranked twenty-first in the state with its producton of 17,252 bales of the fleecy staple.[9]

Among the most prosperous of the immigrants to the new county was a man with the curious name of Beloved Love Turner. B. L., as he was called, was the son of Abner Turner, who was born in Halifax County, Virginia, in 1774, and Chaste Ester Love, whose birthplace was Greene County, Alabama. Abner was fourteen years older than Chaste, and by the time of their marriage in 1806, he had long since left Virginia for the cotton lands of Georgia. After B. L.'s birth the couple moved on southwest to Washington County, Alabama. Their next move was to neighboring Clarke County in 1809. Settling down in the community of West Bend, the Turner family increased—after B. L. they had Andrew Jackson Turner, Boswell Turner, and Virtuous Mary Turner. Abner succeeded as a planter and became a wealthy landowner. B. L.'s educational background is unknown, although as the son of a prosperous and influential man, he undoubtedly had a private tutor and could easily have gone on to college. In 1834 he married Harriet King Mitchell.[10]

Young Turner became a planter, but he also turned

9. *Ibid,* 2–5, 193. *Acts,* 1849, p. 403, specifically designated work on Choctaw County's public roads by such usually exempted persons as county and circuit clerks, sheriffs, justices of the peace, millers, ferrymen, teachers, students, overseers, militia officers, and constables.

10. Genealogical information in the form of charts, family records, and family Bibles were kindly supplied by Mrs. Wayne (Lanelle) Turner and Mrs. Clara Turner of Butler. See Rev. T. H. Ball, *A Glance into the Great South-East, or Clarke County, Alabama, and Its Surroundings, from 1540 to 1877* (Grove Hill, Ala., 1882), 445, 524.

his interests to politics. Well built with a dark complexion and black eyes, he proved himself an attractive and persuasive candidate. He was elected as a Democrat to represent his district in both the state House of Representatives and the Senate in the 1840s. State legislators rarely leave a notable imprint on history, but B. L. at least gained a measure of fame during the 1849 session of the legislature. In December the state capitol was demolished by fire, but B. L., who was on the premises, summoned the aid of a slave, and together the two men hauled the heavy and unwieldy state seal to safety.[11]

Sometime around 1850 B. L. and Harriet moved to Choctaw County. Purchasing property near Mount Sterling, Turner transferred his affluence from one county to another. In 1850 his 400 improved acres and 1,300 unimproved acres had a cash value of $10,000. The value of his livestock—$1,998, most of it represented by 200 swine—was unusually high, although his six bales of cotton did not threaten any production records. Most of Turner's twenty-five hundred bushels of corn were used as food for his family and feed for his livestock.[12]

In the mid-1850s B. L. moved into a large home in Mount Sterling. Curiously (especially in light of his career after the Civil War), he did not extend his farming operations. In fact, Turner evidently sold most of his land. In 1860 his farm comprised only 160 acres and was valued at $6,000. Nor were his 2 horses, 2 mules, 150 swine, and 32 cattle (12 of them milk cows) evidence of impressive wealth. Still, he owned fourteen

11. William Garrett, *Reminiscences of Public Men in Alabama for Thirty Years* (Atlanta, 1872), 430.
12. Agricultural Census, Choctaw County, 1850 (MS in Alabama Department of Archives and History, Montgomery).

slaves.[13] B. L. may have rented additional land or hired out some of his slaves, but, by planter standards he owned little land, and his level of prosperity was on a small scale compared to that typical of the postwar era.

One of Turner's slaves was a robust young man of twenty, named Jack. Where or how B. L. acquired the black is not known. What is known is that Jack was born in Alabama. His black skin covered a muscular six-foot frame, and his powerful physique was given grace and tone by two hundred pounds of flesh. In an objective description, a friend noted later that Jack was "very large and powerfully built," a person "of pure negro blood, with a perfectly black skin." [14]

When the Civil War came the "Ruffin Dragoons" (named for the man who furnished the uniforms) and other Choctaw County units marched off to combat. A number of the county's citizens gave their lives for the Confederacy. On the home front the county suffered from the inconvenience of the blockade, but no battles were fought within its boundaries. B. L., too old for military service, remained at home. With the collapse of the Confederacy, the planter accepted the inevitable and freed Jack and his other slaves. Harriet Turner died in the autumn after the war ended, and B. L. threw himself into what became his life's work—the accumulation of wealth.

13. *Ibid.*
14. See interview with George Turner, a white man, in New York *Times,* August 26, 1882. For another physical description of Jack Turner see Butler *Courier,* September 13 (misprinted as September 16), 1882. The Slave Census, Choctaw County, 1860 (MS in Alabama Department of Archives and History, Montgomery), 42–43, lists B. L.'s slaves by age, sex, and color but not by name. The slave who undoubtedly was Jack is listed as being older than he actually was.

Whatever B. L.'s economic aspirations might have been, they were influenced by politics. In the troubled world of Alabama politics, as in the rest of the South, the pattern that emerged was a somewhat unnatural coalition: old-line Whigs and Democrats forgot traditional animosities and joined forces against the threat posed by the Republicans. The Republican party was formed in Alabama in 1867. While the party attracted blacks and newly arrived Northern whites, a small number of whites, most of them from the Tennessee Valley of north Alabama, also joined. For reasons never disclosed, B. L., who was not a man to explain his actions, made peace with the new order and became a Republican. Such defection earned him the scathing indictment of *scalawag*. If the stigma ever affected him, he did not show it. Instead, he made money. Few Alabamians (and no Choctaw countians) amassed so much wealth during Reconstruction.

After Appomattox the divided nation began the painful and complex process of becoming one again. For the victorious North, the issue was one of adjustment and reorientation to a peacetime economy. Far more desperate and critical was the plight of the South where a way of life had been revolutionized. Whites and blacks faced a situation without precedent, and no area, Choctaw County included, could escape the necessity of planning for the future or the more pressing demand of surviving in the present.

Choctaw County was plunged into the violence and upheaval of Reconstruction. The county, although less turbulent than other sections of the Black Belt, had its share of Ku Klux Klansmen, its portion of Freedman's Bureau agents and Union soldiers vilified as diabolical agents

intent on enriching themselves and making former slaves
the political, economic, and social equals of the native
whites. Corruption, graft, incompetence—white Southerners ticked off their list of accusations against the Republican or Radical regime. In the political battles that followed, the Republicans won temporary victories largely
because of the newly enfranchised Negro voters. In all of
Alabama, the heavily Negro Black Belt became the most
reliable stronghold of the Republican party.

B. L.'s former slave took Turner as his surname and
by the early 1870s emerged as a leader of his race. In
the necessary work of organizing the blacks for political
action, Jack Turner was recognized as a natural leader.
When persuasion and discussion failed to hold those
Negroes fearful of white reprisal in line, Jack was capable of carrying his point through sheer physical domination. It was certain that a black of Jack Turner's presence
would not be ignored in Choctaw County. Democratic
power, temporarily in the ascendancy in 1872, was still
marginal and depended on controlling at least a number
of Negro votes: either by persuading the blacks to vote
Democratic or by persuading them not to vote at all.
A man like Jack Turner who stirred the Negroes to activism—Republican activism—was dangerous.

Besides this, and even more important, there was Jack
Turner, the man. For all his lack of formal education
Jack was perceptive and articulate, an orator capable of
spellbinding power; and this ability, combined with his
prepossessing physical appearance and courage, marked
him for controversy and confrontation. Jack was neither
docile nor servile. As the well-treated slave of B. L.
Turner, he had never known cruelty, and now with the

dignity that accompanied freedom, Jack refused to cower before any man, black or white. If Jack Turner walked with the upright bearing of a person proud of himself and his race, such demeanor was interpreted by many whites as the hateful swagger of a black who did not know his place. The threat he posed as a political leader and his personal traits of self-assurance and independence soon brought him into difficulty with the law.

Jack's activities after 1865, such as the precise date when he took a wife, cannot be chronicled in detail. There is no doubt, however, but that after the Civil War Jack remained in Choctaw County working as a farm laborer in the area of Mount Sterling and Tuscahoma. The manuscript census for 1870 does not contain his name, but that census, the first after the Civil War, was conducted under less than ideal conditions and is grievously inadequate. Jack Turner, like many blacks and numerous whites, simply never was enrolled by the census taker in his "beat" (precinct) or township.

Sometime after the end of the war Jack took a wife, a mulatto woman named Chloe who was four years younger than he. The marriage records in the Choctaw County courthouse offer no evidence that Jack and Chloe applied for a license. If Chloe, who was born in Alabama, was a resident of a neighboring district, her marriage to Jack could have taken place outside of Choctaw County. More likely she was a native of the county. That the former slave woman was attractive is probable, and it is not difficult to understand why she fell in love with the charismatic Jack. They became common-law man and wife, and in 1870 the couple had a daughter whom they named Nelly. Beloved, named for Jack's former master, was born in 1872. Another son, Luther, was born in 1874.[15]

With a wife and a growing family to support, Jack Turner labored as a tenant farmer. While it would have been logical for Jack to work for B. L. Turner, he did not. Yet their friendship deepened in the years of freedom, and B. L. aided and protected Jack. Although the white Turner did not know it and would have been unable to prevent it, his role during Reconstruction had a profound effect on Jack's life. After 1865 B. L. became a moderately active Republican—although never a candidate, Turner did not hide his affiliations or his convictions and on one occasion in 1872 attended a mass public meeting to denounce the night-riding exploits of the Ku Klux Klan [16]—and an extremely active businessman. Buying and selling land, investing in railroads and factories in other parts of the state and the South, B. L. fully developed his entrepreneurial talents. In a period of bitter economic poverty for most, B. L. grew rich. His wealth, which was due mainly to his business ability, was believed by many of his white neighbors to be the result of his connections with Reconstruction authorities. By 1870 B. L.'s personal estate was valued at three thousand dollars, his real estate at fifteen thousand dollars, and from that time on, his holdings were rapidly expanded into a small empire. In 1875 he was the second highest taxpayer in the county.[17]

Although many whites in Choctaw County considered

15.   Population Census, Choctaw County, 1880 (MS in Alabama Department of Archives and History, Montgomery).

16.   Bladon Springs *Herald*, February 9, 1872.

17.   Population Census, Choctaw County, 1870; Choctaw County Tax Book, 1875 (Probate Judge's Office, Choctaw County Courthouse, Butler).

B. L. Turner an apostate and in private conversations expressed their view that he, like other scalawags, had betrayed his people, there was nothing they could do to injure him. He was too powerful; and though his views might be odious, people still deferred, at least publicly, to his wealth. But Jack Turner was another matter. If many whites consciously or subconsciously demanded obsequious behavior from the former bondsman, they were at first disappointed, then frustrated, and finally outraged. Jack Turner became the symbol of their bitter defeat, an intractable black always present to remind them of the new and hated order. Because his former master could flout his Radical ties with impunity, it was not unnatural for whites to transfer their resentment to the arrogant Negro. Thus B. L. became the unwitting and unintentional contributor to the smoldering anger directed against Jack.

Welcoming but not dependent upon the fraternalism of B. L., Jack began the tortured and seemingly impossible task of improving his place in society. He had somehow to employ his intelligence, which was sharp and penetrating despite the absence of any classroom instruction, in a setting that placed no premium on mental exertions by former slaves. His physical endowments qualified him for the role (and there seemed no alternative) of a tenant farmer, but it was not in Jack's nature to accept the status of a lowly sharecropper. He, no less than many whites, had a sense of place and belonging. For Jack Turner the green, rolling land that sometimes turned unexpectedly into soft hills, the rich pastures and dark productive soil, the game-filled woods, and the strings of patternless streams (and always the slate-blue Tombigbee) were his home. As much as anyone, Jack knew and loved the earth and believed that he had the right to share in its bounty. He was free. There was a chance for him and Chloe and the children, or if there were none, no reason for hope, Jack refused to believe it. The most immediate chance lay in politics. The world of Southern politics, Black Belt politics, and most fundamentally, Choctaw County politics, was highly complex and, paradoxically, seemed increasingly complex the more local the arena.

As Jack Turner's profile became that of an emerging political leader, he discovered that his private life, much more than was true of other men, was closely scrutinized by county authorities. Controlling the actions of a man considered undesirable might, if carefully undertaken, be accomplished legally. The law itself could be used as a repressive weapon and with results that were unassailable. Tracing the various charges and trials that Jack faced before the circuit court and county court is a difficult and confusing task. On occasion the same case is entered several times in different official records books, and in a number of instances cases are recorded with no indication of their disposition. Even so, the county's records were more complete and better preserved than those in most of the state's courthouses. A list of Jack's crimes, real and alleged, was prepared by a special Citizens' Committee of Choctaw County in 1882 that, while useful, was neither complete nor accurate. It is certainly true that between 1871 and 1874 Jack Turner appeared frequently before the local courts. Among the charges he faced were gambling, assault and battery with a knife, assault and battery with a stick, and disturbing females by fighting near a place of public worship. He was found innocent of some of the charges, pled innocent but was found guilty of others, and, at times, pled guilty. His fines ranged as low as $5 and never exceeded $20, with B. L. Turner usually serving as his surety.[18]

The Citizens' Committee turned in its special report on Jack Turner in 1882 in an attempt to establish the impression that he was a lawless incorrigible whose unruly background was that of a dangerous, chronic troublemaker. Without denying that Jack Turner had his share of human faults, and admitting that he violated the strict letter of the law more often than most men, it is still true that the majority of his "crimes" were petty. The legal terminology of the charges far exceeded in gravity the peccadillos themselves. Most of the transgressions for which Jack was arrested—drinking, outbursts of temper —were ignored by law officials when committed by others, both black and white. In fact, it is not difficult to conclude that a number of people were anxious to keep Jack under control. When he stepped out of line charges were immediately filed against him. Jack's financial resources were extremely limited, and in the summer of 1873 he had to borrow $80.35 to pay the fines assessed against him. Since the county had no bank, he was forced to arrange the loan by giving a lien on his entire cotton crop.[19]

Yet Jack Turner could not be broken. He had the support of B. L. Turner, and while his former master paid the fines, Jack himself paid something else: his poll

18. See Special Citizens' Report to Governor R. W. Cobb, September 4, 1882, in Butler *Courier,* October 21, 1882; and for examples, Book D, March 28, 1871, p. 833; March 25, 1872, pp. 952–53; Book P, Spring Term, 1872, p. 7; Book C, May 8, 1873, pp. 166–67; and November 6, 1873, p. 230, all on file in the Circuit Clerk's Office, Choctaw County Courthouse.

19. Choctaw County Record of Mortgages, 1873, Probate Judge's Office, Choctaw County Courthouse.

tax. No matter how difficult money was to come by, he regularly went to the courthouse at Butler and paid the $1.50 tax.[20] Payment of the poll tax was not a requirement for voting, although Jack also carefully adhered to the state's regulations concerning voters. By 1874 he was well known throughout Choctaw County—favorably and with respect by most blacks and some whites, unfavorably and with fear by numerous whites. His bouts with the law and his political activities were the subject of numerous conversations. As the dramatic elections of 1874 approached, Jack prepared to take part.

According to the United States Census of 1870, Choctaw County had a population of 6,872 blacks and 5,802 whites. The number of black voters was 1,145.[21] Various means of political intimidation, ranging from economic pressure to physical coercion by White Cappers (the new name assumed by former Klansmen), prevented the Republicans from turning their majority of voters into victory at the polls. In the gubernatorial election of 1872, Republican candidate David P. Lewis carried the state but lost Choctaw County to his Democratic opponent, Thomas H. Herndon, by a vote of 1,177 to 644. Still, the career of Herndon—lawyer, state legislator, Civil War veteran—was far from over.[22]

20. See for example Choctaw County Assessment of Taxes on Real Estate and Personal Property, 1872, Tax Assessor's Office, Choctaw County Courthouse.

21. *Ninth Census, 1870,* Population, I, 11–12. The county had two Indians. The figure of 1,145 black voters, most of whom were Republicans, was given by the partisan (Montgomery) *Alabama State Journal,* October 27, 1874. The estimate was probably accurate.

22. Official Election Returns, Governor's Contest, 1872 (MS in Alabama Department of Archives and History, Montgomery). See also John Z. Sloan, "The Ku Klux Klan and the Alabama Election of 1872," *Alabama Review,* XVIII (April, 1965), 113–23. For sketches of Herndon see Thomas McAdory Owen, *History of Alabama and*

The congressional elections of November, 1872, saw the bitterly hated Charles Hays, a white man and formerly a slave owner from Greene County, carry the Fourth District. Because the district was composed of Black Belt counties, Hays won easily. Yet he lost Choctaw County to Democrat William R. Smith by a vote of almost two to one.[23]

Outside of the Black Belt the Republican power structure was on the verge of collapse as the state organization was weakened by fratricidal difficulties. The party was torn by personal animostities and rivalries between the carpetbag and scalawag elements. The Republican cleavage in Alabama became one of philosophy and geography. In north Alabama, where there were no large concentrations of blacks, the Republicans tended to be hill-country farmers attracted to the party's program of political and social reform and governmental aid for the economic development of their long-neglected area. These small farmers favored a moderate course for the party, one dominated by the whites. They did not champion the cause of the blacks (some white north Alabamians advocated expelling Negroes from the party) and strongly opposed the power wielded by the Black Belt. As the other base of Republican power, the Black Belt was more radical and was controlled by carpetbaggers

Dictionary of Alabama Biography (Chicago, 1921), III, 803; and *Biographical Directory of the American Congress, 1771–1961* (Washington, D.C., 1961), 1046.

23. Official Election Returns, Fourth District Congressional Contest, 1872 (MS in Alabama Department of Archives and History, Montgomery). Hays received 643 votes to Smith's 1,174. The Fourth District's other counties included Marengo, Sumter, Greene, Hale, Perry, Bibb, Autauga, Shelby, Tuscaloosa, Pickens, Lamar, and Fayette. See William Letford (comp.), *Alabama Congressional and Legislative Representation, 1819 to 1860* (Montgomery, [1960?]).

and blacks who wanted to extend the measures begun by
Congress.[24]

Even in the Black Belt, the Negroes, composing the
majority of the Republican party, never enjoyed positions of power commensurate with their contributions.
They were constantly manipulated by white Republican
politicians. At the national level the American people
became weary of stories from the South of profligate
excesses in administration by the Radicals and grotesque
tales of outrages by Southern whites against blacks. The
war was over, and many Americans were willing for Reconstruction to be over as well and for the nation to get
on with building railroads and establishing factories and
expanding its emerging position as an industrial giant.

The well-known result was that in state after state of
the former Confederacy the conservative Democrats re-
gained political control. Soon to be called Bourbons
(carrying the connotation of extreme fiscal and racial
conservatism, the term *Bourbon* is somewhat inaccurate
because it implies a return to agrarian patterns and a re-
jection of industry and manufacturing; in truth many
Bourbons favored industry over agriculture and actively
promoted Northern investments in the South; in this
study the word *Bourbon* applies to those conservative
Democrats and former Whigs who achieved political
dominance in Alabama by preaching retrenchment and
reform in state government and, equally important, white
supremacy), these men organized for a dramatic and
massive overthrow of the Republicans in the elections
of 1874.

24. Allen Johnston Going, *Bourbon Democracy in Alabama,
1874–1890* (University, Ala., 1951), 9; Allen W. Trelease, "Who
Were the Scalawags?" *Journal of Southern History,* XXIX (November, 1963), 445–68.

Meeting at Montgomery in July, delegates to the state convention of conservative Democrats nominated a ticket tailored for victory. It was headed by gubernatorial candidate George Smith Houston of Limestone County in north Alabama. Former Unionist Houston campaigned on a platform of home rule, law and order, economy in government, and white supremacy. The determined Democrats hammered the planks into place and, returning from the state capital, took their issues to the voters as the acrimonious campaign began.[25]

Although technically a part of the safely Republican Black Belt, Choctaw County had gone Democratic in 1872, and the Radicals appeared to have little hope for victory in the upcoming canvass. By ceaseless newspaper bombardments, M. L. Yeatman, who had moved his Bladon Springs *Herald* to Butler and renamed it the *Choctaw Herald,* made the word *Republican* a synonym for corruption and venality. (It is ironical that by 1877 the self-righteous Yeatman had lost his paper, defaulted as postmaster, and fled to Arkansas.[26]) Although a number of conservative Democrats had shared in the economic spoils of Reconstruction (and while other Bourbons in later years would be exposed for corruption in office), they posed as honest men. In Choctaw County as elsewhere, they promised to purge the land of dishonest Radicals. Most of the whites who had dared face social ostracism by becoming Republicans—there had

25. See Edward C. Williamson, "The Alabama Election of 1874," *Alabama Review,* XVII (July, 1964), 210–18; and Walter L. Fleming, *Civil War and Reconstruction in Alabama* (New York, 1905), 771–97.

26. William E. Beggs became editor of the Butler *News* in July, 1876. He renamed his journal the *Choctaw County News* in 1878. In the Butler *News,* August 4, 1877, Editor Beggs referred to Yeatman as "Mr. Skunk," adding "you are an embezler [*sic*], defaulter, deadbeat and liar."

never been many—drifted back into the Democratic party.

Yet there were a number of whites unwilling to accept the Bourbon regime without contest, and across the state and South, Independent movements were spawned. The Independent parties became an odd mixture of idealistic white reformers who objected to Bourbon hegemony, disgruntled politicians who simply wanted the emoluments of office, and whites philosophically opposed to the Democrats but reluctant to become Republicans and accept the automatic brand of endorsing Negro equality and dishonesty in government. Because the Independent movement had neither organization nor a clearly defined philosophy, many whites and blacks were suspect of its alternatives and gave it wary support. Later in the 1870s the Independent organizations merged in some localities (including Choctaw County) with the inflationary Greenback party. In Alabama the Independent and Greenbacker movement became strongest in the white counties of the Tennessee Valley.

As the number of white Republicans declined in Choctaw County, responsibility for maintaining party organization fell increasingly on the blacks. Jack Turner, Edmond Turner (no kin), and Fred Barney, an educated man who taught school near Mount Sterling, became leaders in the Republican party. The relationship between Jack and Fred Barney was extremely close. The young teacher married in 1872, and soon assumed the responsibilities of family life.[27] But his fate and that of Jack Turner, politically and personally, were interlocked.

Jack and other blacks might be disappointed that

27. Marriage Record, Colored, Choctaw County, Book 1, p. 38, Probate Judge's Office, Choctaw County Courthouse.

Republican promises rarely were carried out, but loyalty to the party of Lincoln remained strong. Had there been no Republican party it was difficult to believe that there would be schools for blacks and voting rights for blacks or even personal freedom for blacks. It was true that the educational system was in a shambles and that many inadequately supported schools were closed. But the principle of publicly financed education, no matter how imperfectly implemented, had been pushed by the Republicans, and the Negroes took note. Republicans might be devious, but their chicaneries were infinitely preferable to those of the Bourbons.

2
The Invasion of Butler

In the summer of 1874 Jack Turner and several blacks living near Tuscahoma and Mount Sterling decided to reorganize for a major political effort. Their general strategy was to support the statewide Republican ticket but to work at the local level for the whites who were running as Independents, particularly for Warner Bailey, candidate for probate judge. In order to bring out as many voters as possible for the November elections, Jack and other black leaders held a series of political meetings in private homes in their neighborhood. The Republican congressional convention was scheduled for Uniontown in Perry County on July 29, and the state convention for Montgomery on August 20. The blacks responded to the call, and at the first meeting, held at Edmond Turner's rented place, they agreed to subscribe money to pay their delegates' expenses to and from Montgomery. They also agreed to keep the proceedings of their meetings secret because the Democrats were hostile toward Negro Republicans. To assure the confidential nature of their gatherings, all present agreed that if anyone revealed their political plans he would be punished by whipping.[1] Similar meetings—at Jack Turner's and elsewhere—were held both at night and during the day.

The meetings and their aftermath proved crucial to Jack Turner's future. Certain Democrats, alarmed by what they called the "midnight conspiracies," were determined to turn their alarm into action. The state's leading Democratic paper later charged that Jack Turner and his followers were urged to take violent action by four itinerant blacks who addressed them and then went into Clarke and other counties fomenting trouble. The newspaper pointed out that the blacks planned to organize themselves into companies and seize the growing crops.[2] What they intended to do with the crops once they seized them was not explained.

In a private letter dated September 21, and addressed to Governor Lewis, Jack Turner and Edmond Turner outlined conditions and events in Choctaw County. They explained that the meeting at Edmond Turner's had taken place around August 1, and delegates to the state convention (Jack Turner, Edmond Turner, and Jackson Finley) had been selected. At the local level the Independent candidates were endorsed. The meeting had been strictly political and had in no way advocated racial violence. Shortly after the meeting, whites learned of it and began harassing the blacks. The proceedings had been leaked "through one of our race," and it was not long before certain whites were riding near the homes of

1. Montgomery *Alabama State Journal,* September 16, 1874. The Republican paper was probably accurate, since such stipulations were neither uncommon nor illogical at similar gatherings of blacks in the Reconstruction South.

2. Montgomery *Advertiser,* October 3, 1874.

both Turners and threatening them with physical harm
if they took an active part in the campaign. "Colored
men have been assaulted, threatened, driven from their
homes and families," the governor was informed, "and
otherwise maltreated, simply because they had expressed
their desire to support Republican candidates." Because
of his open support of Warner Bailey for judge of probate
"Jack Turner . . . was notified that he must never
'show his face in Choctaw county again.' " [3]

Huff Cheney, a Negro who lived at Tuscahoma and
was employed by a white man, was exposed as the in-
former. What embellishments, if any, Cheney added are
not known, although the mere fact of blacks meeting together was enough to alarm some whites and result in
action designed to disrupt the meetings. In any case, the
blacks were soon aware of Cheney's indiscretions and
held a meeting where it was decided to impose the punishment agreed to previously. On Saturday, August 8, a
gathering of blacks at Tuscahoma carried out the sentence: Huff Cheney was taken from his house, marched
into the nearby Tombigbee swamp, and given a whipping.[4]

The severity of the act depended upon who recounted
it. The Negroes, a group of forty, were described by a
Democratic journal as "black fiends in human shape." [5]
They had, the newspaper insisted, inflicted upon Cheney's

3. Jack Turner and Edmond Turner to David P. Lewis in David
P. Lewis Papers, Alabama Department of Archives and History,
Montgomery. Of the various letters and statements made about the
"invasion," this letter is clearly the most reliable. For more on Governor Lewis, an educated native Alabamian who had opposed seces-
sion, see Sarah Van V. Woolfolk, "Five Men Called Scalawags,"
Alabama Review, XVII (January, 1964). 45–55.
4. Montgomery *Alabama State Journal*, September 16, 1874.
5. Butler *Choctaw Herald*, August 26, 1874.

"person corporal punishment to the tune of about six hundred lashes, and then informed him, as a reminder, that if he reported on them they would take his life." [6] The same paper said that Cheney had "received at the hands of these inhuman wretches, one of the most brutal floggings that was ever inflicted on a human being. He was divested of every particle of clothing, and as many of the savage scoundrels as could crowd around him, participated in the inhuman performance." [7] Why had they done it? According to the Bourbon journal, "The excuse they gave him for the hellish deed was that he had given the white men an insight to their midnight conspiracies." [8] Put briefly and dramatically, Cheney had been "scourged nigh unto death." [9]

The state newspaper for the Republican party declared that Huff Cheney, when confronted with the charges, admitted them, consented to the whipping, and once it had been administered, asked to be reinstated in the blacks' councils. As for the punishment, Cheney was "whipped—not immoderately or unmercifully, as charged, but really and truly whipped." [10]

After the punitive action Cheney once again reported to the whites what had happened. The *Choctaw Herald* denied that the black had agreed to be whipped, asserting that he had not criticized the men who punished him and

6. Montgomery *Alabama State Journal*, August 26, 1874, quoting Butler *Choctaw Herald*, August 12, 1874.
7. Butler *Choctaw Herald*, August 19, 1874.
8. *Ibid.*, August 12, 1874, quoted in Montgomery *Alabama State Journal*, August 26, 1874.
9. Butler *Choctaw Herald*, August 26, 1874. The most one-sided and inaccurate account of the whipping and the incidents that followed may be found in the pro-Democratic Selma *Echo*, quoted in Livingston *Journal*, August 28, 1874.
10. Montgomery *Alabama State Journal*, September 16, 1874.

was afraid to leave home because he anticipated an attempt on his life.[11] It was bad enough for the blacks to organize politically, but if Jack Turner and others were permitted to break the law and, equally undesirable, control black voters, Choctaw County's recent Democratic victories might be reversed. Indignant at what had happened and fearful of what it portended, county officials made preparations to arrest Jack and any others implicated in the whipping. On August 12 Deputy Sheriff Edward A. Glover (who had been acting sheriff for several months) received a warrant from Justice of the Peace H. L. Glover for the arrest of Jack Turner and nineteen other blacks. They had breached the peace of the state by participating in the "lynching" of Huff Cheney. In legal terms lynching amounted to any form of corporal punishment administered by a mob. The stage was set for the "Invasion of Butler."

On the morning of August 13, Deputy Sheriff Glover and a posse of five men (W. Turnbow, George Dill, James Marshal, Mit Roach, and William Curtis) left Butler for Mount Sterling to execute the warrant. By chance the posse encountered Jack Turner walking along the road. He was armed with a shotgun and a pistol.[12] As an acknowledged leader of his race and having been involved in the Cheney affair, Jack had obviously anticipated some retributive action. There was no law against

11. *Choctaw Herald*, September 23, 1874.
12. See Address of the Democratic State Executive Committee, issued from Montgomery, Alabama, October 1, 1874, hereinafter cited as Executive Committee Address. Accompanying the address were a number of affidavits, including that of Glover. The address was widely reprinted, and may for convenience be found in Butler *Choctaw Herald*, October 14, 1874. The regular sheriff had resigned in March because he did not believe he could preserve order. See Bladon Springs *Herald*, April 12, 1874.

carrying arms, and it was common practice, especially for white men, to keep weapons almost as casual companions.

Glover informed Turner of the warrant, stating that he had to appear that day in county court before Judge J. S. Evans. According to Glover, Turner replied, "I don't know about that." Glover next filled out an appearance bond and claimed later that Jack refused to sign it until the lawman threatened to take him to jail immediately.[13] The bond required Jack to answer a charge of lynching, "that is to say, abusing, whipping or beating one Huff Cheney" because he "had been disclosing certain acts" of Edmond Turner and others.[14] Jack was not disarmed, and the posse rode on toward Mount Sterling to issue the other warrants.

The Negro leader followed on foot and a short time later caught up with the posse at the schoolhouse where they were serving a warrant on Fred Barney. Glover maintained that when Jack appeared he became angry and dispatched a Negro schoolboy to the nearby Catlin plantation and Ridgeway place. Jack instructed the lad to tell the men concerned with the Huff Cheney matter to arm themselves and meet him at Tom King's. He also wanted the names of all who refused to come. As recounted by Glover, Jack said, "By God this is as good a time to die and go to hell as any other." [15]

Having taken care of Fred Barney, the posse con-

13. Glover's affidavit in Executive Committee Address.
14. Appearance Bond, August 13, 1874, Circuit Clerk's Office, Choctaw County Courthouse. Besides Jack Turner, Edmond Turner, and Fred Barney the bond named the following men: Jim Barnett, Joe Ford, John Turner, Joe Chastang, Ike Mingo Turner, William Burgess, Aleck Turner, Harrison Barney, Mark Turner, Lorenzo Ward, Allen King, and Range West.
15. Glover's affidavit in Executive Committee Address.

tinued its journey to Mount Sterling. Glover said he saw
Jack later at Tom King's with eight or ten armed men.
Then within an hour, while the posse was at a house on
the Mount Sterling road, Glover saw Jack Turner pass
by with a party of twenty-five Negroes, most of them
armed.[16] According to Jack he was accompanied by
about twenty men, some of whom had been served warrants to appear in court. Others were friends anxious for
the safety of the men charged. Jack said that some of the
men were armed with shotguns and muskets, but that
only he had a pistol.[17]

Why were Jack Turner and his men carrying weapons?
To the *Choctaw Herald* the answer was simple: "Jack
and his crowd armed themselves . . . to 'clean out the
Court.' They refused to be tried by the courts of this
State or by the County Court, and said that Bill Jones
[United States Commissioner William Jones, whose headquarters were at Demopolis, Marengo County] had informed them that the U.S. authorities alone had jurisdiction over their case." [18] In refutation, a Republican editor noted that on the morning the sheriff's posse appeared
in Mount Sterling, Cheney announced his intention of
taking his double-barreled shotgun, going to court at
Butler, and shooting every black who had participated in
punishing him. Cheney also had a number of relatives,
and his threats, coupled with the possibility of kinfolk
allies, caused Jack and his men to carry guns to protect
themselves.[19] Jack Turner later explained that Huff
Cheney had boasted of having whites on his side and of
his determination to be revenged upon his enemies that

16. *Ibid.*
17. Turner's affidavit, *ibid.*
18. Butler *Choctaw Herald,* September 23, 1874.
19. Montgomery *Alabama State Journal,* September 16, 1874.

day. Self-protection, Jack Turner declared, was the only reason he and his men carried weapons.[20]

Deputy Sheriff Glover swore that prior to seeing Jack Turner's force of blacks pass by, he encountered Huff Cheney who was on his way to Mount Sterling. Fearing that Turner's men would harm Cheney, Glover and the posse overtook the procession of accused blacks, passed them, and cantered into the village. When they reached Mount Sterling, Glover stationed four of his men there and with the remaining member of the posse rode back to Butler. The horses, heavily lathered from the hard ride in the summer heat, reached Butler before noon. Glover explained his haste: "I anticipated trouble from Jack." Glover quickly made the morning's events known. Because of county court and a called meeting of the Grange, the small town contained an unusually large number of men. Even if Sheriff Glover had told his story in understated tones (and the Montgomery *Alabama State Journal* accused him of spreading "the most incendiary report as to the purposes and objects of the negroes" [21]), it is not difficult to imagine the reaction.

J. W. Bruister, a leading citizen, said word was received "that Jack Turner was coming into town with a company of armed negroes, and that he intended mischief"; [22] a more critical source avowed that "Immediately every man in the town who could raise a shot gun, or a pistol, rushed out to repel the imaginary armed invasion." [23] In any event, the townsmen agreed that some older men should go out to meet the blacks, ascertain

20. Turner's affidavit in Executive Committee Address.
21. Montgomery *Alabama State Journal*, September 16, 1874; Glover's affidavit in Executive Committee Address.
22. Bruister's affidavit in Executive Committee Address.
23. Montgomery *Alabama State Journal*, September 16, 1874.

their intentions, and endeavor to pacify them. Bruister, A. J. Gray, Ed McCall, and J. E. Scott were delegated to confer with Jack. The other men in town secured arms, and, according to Glover, "several fired off their guns to reload them." [24]

In short order Jack and his men, now increased to thirty and carrying weapons, were sighted approaching the town. The perspiring men paused about half a mile from Butler where they were met by Bruister and the three other men, all unarmed. As Bruister described the confrontation, he asked Jack what he and the others intended. Jack replied that he had been summoned to court and was going in. Bruiser urged him not to lead the armed men into town because there would be trouble. But, in Bruister's words, Jack "said they were going just in that way, that the white people had had the law and courts all their own way, and the colored men now intended to have their rights; that a law had been passed guaranteeing them their rights; that if all should be arrested who had been concerned in whipping Huff Cheney, he was willing to be tried; but that those of them who had been arrested should not be tried without the others." Bruister said that Jack "showed a great deal of temper, swore frequently, and impressed strongly with the belief that he intended to use force in maintaining his views." [25]

About this time Deputy Sheriff Glover emerged from town and joined the conferring parties. He remained long enough to inform the blacks that those who had been arrested had to attend court, and then he returned to Butler. Jack maintained that he told Bruister and the others that he was merely obeying the summons and in-

24. Glover's affidavit in Executive Committee Address.
25. Bruister's affidavit, *ibid.*

tended to have his men deposit their arms in John Eddy's shop. He was emphatic in declaring that he had no intention of resisting the law.[26]

Complying with Glover's order, the party of blacks, accompanied by Bruister and the three other whites, moved slowly toward Butler. The blacks, seeing the armed crowd more clearly as they drew nearer, halted. At this point the four-man posse (enlarged now to nine), which had left Mount Sterling for Butler, made an appearance. Jack and his men were caught between the townsmen whom they faced and the posse to their rear. The August sun brought the drama into sharp, tense focus.

There is no reason to doubt that regardless of his peaceful intentions and declarations, Jack Turner had greatly frightened the whites. Deputy Sheriff Glover's warnings seemed capable of realization as the men in Butler watched the armed band of Negroes approach. Yet Jack was not coming to Butler of his own free will but because he had been arrested and ordered to and would have been breaking the law had he not done so. But this logic was forgotten in the tension of the moment.

If the whites were apprehensive, what about the blacks? Huff Cheney had issued threats and boasted of having white support, several of their number had been arrested, and they had been commanded to come to town to face whatever justice was waiting. The crowd of armed white men posed an ominous threat of possible attack. Fear turned to panic when the posse rode up behind, and one by one the Negroes left the road disappearing into the woods.

Even Jack Turner's most bitter enemies never doubted

26. Turner's affidavit, *ibid.*

his courage. The black man—posed sentinellike in the center of the sandy road—stood his ground refusing to bolt. He urged the others to stand firm and follow him into Butler. But the frightened Negroes could not be rallied, and suddenly the humid stillness was broken by the staccato sound of bullets. Jack turned aside quickly and escaped into the forest. White witnesses and participants later claimed that the gunfire was sporadic, while Jack and the blacks admitted the whites had not laid down a steady fusillade but insisted that many rounds were fired. Regardless of the number of shots, no one was killed or injured.[27] What would become known as the "Invasion of Butler" was over in a matter of moments.

The arrest warrants had been served but the confrontation at Butler's outskirts had forestalled any trial. During the days between August 13 and August 20, when the Republican state convention convened, Jack Turner and the other accused men went into hiding. There were reports that the blacks had crossed the Tombigbee into Marengo County and raised a force of 200 men to resist the whites. The militant blacks were supposedly bivouacked south of Nanafalia. Deputy Sheriff Glover received a warrant for the rearrest of the leaders. He raised a posse of 150 men and went to the river, where he received additional men and assistance from the sheriff of Marengo County. On August 19 the posse, which had

27. See affidavits of Turner, Bruister (whose statements were countersigned by several whites and three blacks), and Jack Finley, *ibid.* See also Montgomery *Alabama State Journal,* August 26, September 16, 1874. Details of the "invasion" were also taken from an alleged confession of Jack Turner, discussed below, that appeared as a letter in the Montgomery *Advertiser,* August 27, 1874.

become a small army, searched the area of the alleged bastion but found no trace of the blacks.[28]

Another story gaining circulation contended that Jack had 40 men at his command and intended to whip several blacks in the county. If it were not heinous enough to turn on his own people, Jack Turner supposedly was trying to enlist 15 or 20 more men to aid him in lashing his former master, B. L. Turner.[29] It was further reported that "A large body of armed negroes have been encamped . . . on B. [L.] Turner's plantation just across the Bigbee river from Tuscahoma."[30] No one paused to question why such a band—if the plan was to punish the white Turner—would camp openly on his land. That there was an encampment is certain, but the gathering was at most political. No overt acts of violence occurred.

Conjuring fears of pre–Civil War slave insurrections, the *Choctaw Herald* sounded a worried alarm: "Recently the peace and safety of the white people of this county have been seriously and dangerously threatened by warlike demonstrations on the part of the negroes."[31] The *Alabama State Journal,* however, did not permit the *Herald's* statement to pass uncontested. The Republican paper called into question the Butler journal's assertion that Jack Turner and his men had demonstrated a "willingness to inaugurate literally a war between the races." Since Jack had been arrested, shot at while attempting to surrender, and was on the run, the war ap-

28. Glover's affidavit in Executive Committee Address; Montgomery *Advertiser,* August 19, 1874, quoting Selma *Echo.* The *Echo* raised the estimated number of Negro revolutionaries to somewhere between three hundred and four hundred.
29. Butler *Choctaw Herald,* August 19, 1874.
30. *Ibid.*
31. *Ibid.,* August 26, 1874.

peared rather one-sided, and it seemed clear there were "men who are clamoring for his blood!" [32]

When Jack left Choctaw County for the Republican convention at Montgomery, his status was that of a fugitive. Any good-byes to his wife and family were of necessity clandestine and hurried. The newspaper at Butler did not doubt that he was going to "headquarters" to confer with Charles Hays, "Congressional ass from this district." [33]

During this period a curious letter appeared in a Radical newspaper, the Selma *Republican*. The text was released by the man to whom the letter was written, United States Commissioner W. B. Jones. Jack Turner and five other men were the apparent authors of the letter which was written from Mount Sterling, dated August 13, and delivered to Jones at Demopolis. The six men wondered:

> Shall we colored Republicans be killed out again by the Kuklux? The white gentlemen have killed some ten of our men this day, 13th August. We have to defend ourselves. The Democrats say that not a Radical shall vote in Choctaw in November. What shall we do? Please do come down and investigate the matter as a United States officer. We colored people are not afraid of searching for the truth. We assembled at Jack Turner's to have a peaceful political meeting; had no idea of any distrubance until pistols were fired at us by the white people.
>
> Your friends.[34]

The letter was obviously untrue. No blacks had been killed, and it is not likely that on August 13, under the pressure of pursuit, Jack and the others sat down and

32. Montgomery *Alabama State Journal*, August 28, 1874.
33. Butler *Choctaw Herald*, August 18, 1874.
34. For a reprinting of the letter, see Montgomery *Alabama State Journal*, August 23, 1874. The other signatories were Bengay Wood, Joe Turner, Ben Sikes, William Sikes, and Ned. Bush.

wrote a letter to Commissioner Jones. The Montgomery *Advertiser* speculated that the letter was actually written in the state capitol during the Republican state convention, but the city's Republican journal promptly ridiculed the theory.[35] None of the signatures, save that of Jack Turner, had appeared on the list sought by Deputy Sheriff Glover. Nevertheless, the letter was widely reprinted across the state, first by Republican editors convinced of its contents and later by Democratic organs to show how the Radicals levied irresponsible charges. "It is a stinking Radical lie," fumed Editor Yeatman of the *Choctaw Herald*. The story was "manufactured by some white scoundrel with a black heart, for party purposes. We believe [it] was gotten up without the knowledge of the negroes whose names are appended." [36] The paper hinted strongly that William A. "Buck" Lipscomb, a white Republican leader in Marengo County, might have been responsible for the letter. It was certainly true that Jack Turner and his followers were at political odds with Lipscomb. Perhaps Lipscomb resented Jack's leadership, but in any case, the white Republican joined the attempt to arrest the accused Negroes.[37] Editor Yeatman was correct, at least to the extent of his assertion that the names were forged.

Jack Turner, still facing an arrest warrant, went to Demopolis and caught the train to Montgomery to attend the Radical convention. The contents of the sensational letter to Commissioner Jones were immediately made known to the 120 assembled delegates. The raucous con-

35. Montgomery *Advertiser*, August 25, 1874; Montgomery *Alabama State Journal*, August 28, 1874.

36. Butler *Choctaw Herald*, August 26, 1874.

37. *Ibid.* See also Livingston *Journal*, August 28, 1874, quoting Demopolis *Marengo News-Journal*.

viviality usually evident at political conventions was strangely absent as the delegates, conscious of their upcoming fight for survival, were shocked by affairs in Choctaw County as revealed in the stark letter released by Commissioner Jones.

Jack Finley, a black delegate to the convention, spent considerable time buttonholing delegates and assuring them that no massacre of Negroes in Choctaw County had occurred. There was even a widely believed rumor that Jack Turner himself had been killed, or at least wounded. Finley located Jack who agreed to circulate more than usual to reassure his fellow Republicans that he was alive.[38] The *Alabama State Journal,* which at first had believed the letter and demanded a full-scale investigation by federal authorities, was plainly embarrassed.[39] Editor Arthur Bingham sought out Jack Turner on August 21, and in an interview learned that there had been no killings. The editor tried to regain lost face by arguing that since several of the blacks had not been heard from, the natural assumption was that they had been shot.[40]

While the letter to Commissioner Jones was occupying so much editorial attention, the Montgomery *Advertiser* produced what it called Jack Turner's "confession." How the paper procured the statement, which was sent "to a gentleman of this city," was never explained. In the brief statement Jack described how "a negro named Huff betrayed some of our secrets to the white people, and we took him out and whipped him." Jack outlined his own arrest, the episode at Butler (where "white men shot at

38. Finley's affidavit in Executive Committee Address.
39. Montgomery *Alabama State Journal,* August 23, 26, 1874.
40. *Ibid.,* August 28, 1874.

the crowd; I think I was shot at three times"), and re-counted his trip to Montgomery. Jack admitted "No one had been killed when I left. But I helped to write a letter to U.S. Commissioner Jones, in which it was stated that men had been killed. I did that in order to have men sent down to protect me against harm, in consequence of the part I had taken against Huff." [41]

Jack Turner did not concede the truth of the *Advertiser*'s revelation, and the "gentlemen of this city" to whom it was addressed never revealed his identity. It seems probable that the *Advertiser*'s "confession" was no more authentic than the letter to Commissioner Jones. Both letters illustrate how sensational news stories were used to serve political purposes. In a sworn statement, made later while waiting to be tried in the Huff Cheney matter, Jack denied writing a letter to U.S. Commissioner Jones, declared the bogus letter's contents untrue, and maintained that his name had been forged. On his way to the state convention the Negro met Commissioner Jones and informed him of the falsity of the letter. Once at Montgomery, Jack enlarged his clarification: he contacted Congressman Hays and told him that no blacks had been killed or injured. [42]

After participating in the state convention which re-nominated Governor Lewis on a platform calling for law and order and civil and political but not social equality, Jack Turner returned to Choctaw County. He was able to elude capture with relative ease, yet he knew that regardless of the consequences, he and the others were fugitives and had at some point to face trial. Surrendering to

41. Montgomery *Advertiser,* August 27, 1874; see *ibid.,* August 25, 1874.
42. Turner's affidavit in Executive Committee Address.

county authorities did not seem safe or wise, but there was no alternative. "We understand," Editor Yeatman wrote, "that 'Capt. Jack' Turner . . . is very anxious to place himself in the custody of the sheriff, but pretends he is afraid to do so, lest he might suffer violence at the hands of the whites." The incredulous editor added, "This is about the first time we ever heard of Jack being afraid of anything; he has generally been regarded as a stranger to fear." The journalist assured Jack that he would suffer no harm. "The whites have no desire nor intention of harming him, and . . . he can come up at any time without danger of being molested. And when he does come, we hope Jack will be kind enough to show us the graves of those nine colored men who were recently killed in our country. Most people about here are slow to believe that anybody was even wounded, and as Jack made the statement in a published letter he ought to feel sufficiently interested in the vindication of his veracity to show us the place where these men were buried." [43]

Taunts from the *Choctaw Herald* had little effect on Jack Turner. He had ample justification for a careful evaluation of the merits of surrender. While in Montgomery he and fellow Choctaw County delegate Edmond Turner wrote a confidential letter (parts of which have been previously cited) to Governor Lewis. The letter, which never reached public print, described events of the previous weeks in Choctaw County and was signed by both men in bold script signatures. Up to that time Jack Turner had always designated his name with his mark, and it seems likely that the letter was written as the two

43. Butler *Choctaw Herald,* September 9, 1874.

men dictated it. There is later evidence that Jack learned to write his name and probably to read.

The two Turners stated that "at the present time, not less than ten able bodied colored men are absolutely seeking protection in the swamps of the Tombigbee river, their lives having been threatened." Their families were alone and their crops untended. In the past several days numerous white men of Mount Sterling and the vicinity had ridden through the neighborhood taking guns away from the blacks on the pretext that they feared an insurrection. Matters had reached a crisis: "The colored people are actually in such a state of fear that life itself is almost insupportable. We cannot have our churches, our schools, nor any social intercourse with each other, unless watched and insulted by white men. We are not permitted to own guns to protect our premises from intruders, or our crops from destruction by beasts and birds." In a final paragraph the authors acknowledged that the governor's power to provide the protection they needed was limited. Pointing to their previous loyalty to the Republican party, the two men concluded with a request: "We trust that your Excellency will use your great influence to secure us, at least, in the enjoyment of our rights of life and property." [44]

The situation in Choctaw County as well as in Greene, Sumter, and other counties in his district spurred Congressman Hays into action. As a native Southerner and former slaveholder, Hays, by his conversion to the Republican party, was considered a contemptible scalawag. Such an evaluation by his former friends was hardly ob-

44. Jack Turner and Edmond Turner to Lewis in Lewis Papers. See Glover's affidavit in executive committee address for a denial that he or anyone else had disarmed the blacks.

jective, and a scholarly assessment of his career is badly
needed. Hays faced the problem of reelection, and, considered pragmatically, victory was impossible if a large
number of Negro voters were intimidated. The most
effective way to see that black voters cast ballots and that
their votes were counted as cast was to have federal
troops at the polls. Hays had somehow to convince
President Grant, Secretary of War W. W. Belknap, Attorney General George H. Williams, and other federal
authorities that soldiers were actually needed.

To this end, the congressman, along with Republicans
from other Southern states, went to Washington for a
series of conferences. On September 3, 1874, a letter
was sent out from Attorney General Williams authorizing
United States marshals and attorneys to send troops to
designated places.[45] Hays, meanwhile, made no denial of
Democratic accusations that his trip to the capitol was
designed solely to secure the deployment of troops to the
Black Belt.[46] In late August, "Buck" Lipscomb, the white
Republican from Marengo County, was overheard predicting that soon 250 bluecoats would be in Choctaw
County.[47]

Desiring to arouse public attention and gain subsequent action, Congressman Hays wrote a letter on September 7, to Joseph R. Hawley, prominent Republican
editor of the Hartford, Connecticut, *Courant*. Hawley

45. Letter from Attorney General George H. Williams, September 3, 1874 (Microcopy 666, Roll 169, National Archives Publications). Democratic newspapers denounced the action, but Republican
journals were pleased. See Montgomery *Alabama State Journal*,
September 4, 1874.
46. See Butler *Choctaw Herald*, September 23, 1874.
47. *Ibid.*, August 26, 1874. Lipscomb's semipublic statement was
made on the deck of the *Lotus,* a steamer that plied the waters of the
Tombigbee.

was as well a politician, a former abolitionist, and as a Union general had been a commander in the South during the earlier phases of Reconstruction. In his letter Hays made various charges—some true, some stretching the truth, and some entirely false. His sensational allegations were reprinted in the North and South in Democratic and Republican journals. Recounting outrages in several Alabama counties, Hays included Choctaw: fabricated stories of a Negro uprising in Choctaw County, he alleged, were circulated about August 1, and hundreds of whites had hurried to the scene to prevent it. Although no armed blacks could be located, "Yet something must be done to make an example. So a company of whites ambushed a party of negroes returning from church, killed ten and wounded thirteen." [48] Hays's letter, a collage of several events, was untrue.

An infuriated Democratic state executive committee, chaired by Walter L. Bragg, immediately went into action collecting evidence to disprove Hays's statements. On October 1 the executive committee met at Montgomery and issued an address, "To the People of the United States." The document was a lengthy point-by-point refutation of Hays's assertions. From this report emerged the sworn affidavits of Deputy Sheriff Glover, J. W. Bruister, Jack Turner, and others relating their versions of the "Invasion of Butler."

The Democratic committee's address was every bit as politically slanted as that of Hays. Besides dealing in specifics, the address pointed out that Alabama's Republican party was composed largely of blacks, whereas the

48. For a reprinting of Hays's letter to Hawley see Montgomery *Advertiser,* September 22, 1874, but for the original printing see Hartford (Conn.) *Courant,* September 15, 1872.

conservative Democratic party was made up "almost exclusively of the white people of the State embracing a majority of the people." The address acknowledged that in most of the country Republicans were respectable persons who had honest differences with Democrats. But the Republican party in Alabama was different. "The negroes forming nine-tenths of the party here, are of course as a body ignorant, and from their recent condition of slavery a low order of morality prevails among them." Such a situation was lamentable, but worse yet, "The remainder of the party is made up chiefly of professional politicians and their hangers-on, who live by office, and a few worthy people who have been induced heretofore to act with the Republican party. This little army of office holders, with a few honorable exceptions, feels that the contest is one for their dailey bread, and though 'work they will not' yet they are not ashamed to 'beg,' steal, or to lie." [49]

By this time even the closest and most intelligent observer of Choctaw County had every reason to be confused by the tangled chain of events. Most people, white and black, either found the situation hopelessly unfathomable or dismissed everything that was happening as "politics." But for those who had something at stake, recapitulation was in order. Several contradictory letters and documents relating to Choctaw County had been issued: the forged letter supposedly written by Jack Turner and others on August 13, to Commissioner Jones; Jack Turner's so-called "confession" of lying reprinted August 27; the uncirculated private letter of Jack Turner and Edmond Turner to Governor Lewis, dated August 21; the letter written September 7, from Hays to Hawley

49. See Executive Committee Address.

containing largely unsubstantiated charges; and finally, the address of Alabama's Democratic state executive committee of October 1.

At the personal level Jack Turner, intensely aware of the swirl around him, had his own survival and the well-being of his family to consider. The upcoming election of November 3 had become a bitter local and statewide showdown between the Democrats and the coalition Republican and Independent forces—an editorial in the *Choctaw Herald* of September 2 declared, "We are now upon the very threshold of this important contest for white supremacy over negro inferiority and radical rotteness." If the election were fairly conducted, the efforts of Jack Turner and others might pay off in victory. There can be little doubt that Jack strongly supported the efforts to have federal troops present at the polling places.

Although Hays and others had exaggerated their case, there clearly was cause to fear that blacks would not be permitted to exercise a free ballot in several parts of the Black Belt (and isolated areas in other sections). Implementation of Attorney General Williams' letter of September 3 followed within a week, and in all some 430 troops were sent to eight outposts in Alabama, including Butler.[50] Orders went through the various channels, finally sifting down from Major General Irwin McDowell, commander of the Division of the South, with headquarters at Louisville, Kentucky, to Fort McPherson near Atlanta, Georgia. There First Lieutenant Augustus R.

---

50. Most of the troops were dispatched to the Black Belt. Besides Butler, places where units were sent included Mt. Vernon, Livingston, Carrollton, Huntsville, Demopolis, Montevallo, and Eufaula. Letter from Williams, September 3, 1874, National Archives Publication. See also James E. Sefton. *The United States Army and Reconstruction, 1865–1877* (Baton Rouge, 1967), 262.

Egbert, commanding officer of Company I, Second Infantry Regiment, no doubt had misgivings when he read Special Order No. 14, dated September 10. He and his men were ordered to Choctaw County. Atlanta, although still rebuilding from the destructive fire of November, 1864, was, compared to Butler, like Paris. At one time the county seat had boasted an inn, but it burned in 1872, and the only hotel in the entire county was at Bladon Springs. With the exception of C. A. Spangenberg, who had a "house of entertainment" (later known as Butler Hotel) with limited accommodations for food and lodging, visitors were dependent upon the kindness of the people.[51]

Lieutenant Egbert informed his second-in-command, Second Lieutenant William V. Wolfe, of the order, and the company made hurried preparations to depart. Not altogether enthusiastically the two officers, a first sergeant, four other sergeants, a corporal, two "trumpeters," and thirty-five privates boarded a train headed west and began a long journey of 306 miles. The train rattled across Georgia into Alabama and on to Montgomery. From there it cut through the heart of the Black Belt. Lieutenant Egbert and his men gathered their gear and, glad to gain relief from the cramped quarters of the coach, detrained at York Station in Sumter County on the morning of September 15. They had breakfast at eight o'clock and shortly afterwards assembled their wagons and began a forced march of 38 miles to Butler.

51. Returns from Regular Army Infantry Regiments, June 1821–December, 1966 (Microcopy 665, Roll 22, National Archives Publications). See also Egbert's account of his tour in Choctaw County. He wrote it under the name of "Monmouth," and published it in *Forest and Stream*. His article was reprinted in Butler *Choctaw Herald,* February 24, 1875.

Only by the most charitable use of the word could their route be described as a road.[52]

That night the weather turned crisp and cool. About eleven o'clock as the last strains from a violin died softly, a number of young men and women emerged from a dance at the academy in Butler, discussing, no doubt, the latest steps and predicting an early winter. The bantering stopped suddenly as though frozen in the chilly air: before them on the courthouse square in various postures and poses of exhaustion was a company of United States soldiers, complete with a commanding officer. The rumors were true. There were considerably fewer troops than the 250 "Buck" Lipscomb had predicted, but there was no denying the physical presence of the hated yankees. The men of Butler quickly escorted the ladies to their homes and returned to the square. It would have been difficult not to feel some pity for the troops who hardly gave the appearance of heartless mercenaries. They had not eaten since leaving York Station, and as time passed the holes in the road had become craters as they labored to push their wagons up every hill. After night fell they had lighted pitch pine torches and stumbled through the dark forests into town. As Lieutenant Egbert wrote, the men "were pretty well used up . . . [some] so tired out that they would not even build a fire to make themselves some coffee." When the commander asked where his men could get something to eat and a place to sleep he was told that no arrangements were available. Having satisfied their curiosity, the townsmen went their separate ways, angry at the unwelcome intrusion but unable to prevent it.[53]

52. "Monmouth" in *Forest and Stream.*
53. *Ibid.*

A famished Lieutenant Wolfe spied a store door open, entered the building, and appropriated two cans of oysters and two cans of sardines. He and his superior supped on the canned seafood, their thirst slaked, but not pleasantly, by what Egbert described as "execrable water" from the courthouse square's public well. The enlisted men laid their blankets on the ground and fell on them, their hunger forgotten as sleep came quickly. The next morning reveille was supplied by one of the trumpeters, and the rat-tat-tat of a drum set things going. After cooking breakfast from their own provisions, the soldiers went into camp. Their primary duty was to insure the holding of a fair election.[54]

Jack Turner watched the troops go into bivouac with relief. Their presence would make it difficult for his enemies to undertake an act of open violence against him. He gave up his furtive visits in the middle of the night to see Chloe and the children and abandoned his hideouts in the swamps and in the homes of friends. He and the others for whom warrants had been issued turned themselves in to the county authorities. The fugitive's act provoked a sneer from the local editor: "We have no idea that Capt. Jack would have surrendered himself to the custody of the sheriff but for the fact that federal troops have been stationed at this place—Jack no doubt believed that the soldiers were sent here for his especial protection, in response to his lying letter to Bill Jones not long ago, and they would not suffer him to be sent to prison." [55]

The charges were dropped against most of the blacks accused of lynching Huff Cheney. Late in September five

54. *Ibid.*
55. Butler *Choctaw Herald,* September 23, 1874.

were tried, convicted, and fined five hundred dollars each. But Jack Turner, Lorenzo Ward, and several others demanded a trial by jury. Their bail was set at one thousand dollars each, an amount none could raise, and they remained in jail waiting for the next grand jury to convene. As for the convicted blacks, the local paper remarked, "We hope the fate of these negroes will prove a wholesome lesson to the colored people." [56] The meaning of this statement was crystal clear.

That considerable legal maneuvering was taking place is revealed in the motion docket of the circuit court, Choctaw County. During the fall term, 1874, Jack Turner and the others—Isaac Turner, Joe Turner, and Lorenzo Ward—asked the court for a change of venue. The defendants wanted the case moved to the nearest county. In a separate case Jack was charged with a felony: he had failed to answer to a bond in a misdemeanor case.[57] Evidently the latter charge stemmed from his failure to come into Butler on August 13. Warren Bailey, Independent candidate for probate judge, served as the defendant's lawyer in both cases. Cited as justifications for the request were the widespread prejudice in Choctaw County against Jack and the newspaper articles that had been calculated to create a bad image of him. Strangely, the page (45) in the motion docket requesting the change of venue was marked through, but in any case, the request was not granted.

With guilty verdicts already passed against some of the participants in the "Invasion of Butler" and with Jack Turner and others still in jail waiting trial, many blacks

56. *Ibid.*
57. See Motion Docket, Circuit Court, Choctaw County, Commencing with the Fall Term, 1871, Circuit Clerk's Office.

in Choctaw County became despondent and declined to participate, at least openly, in the campaign. Lieutenant Egbert's apprehensions, if he had any, soon vanished when he encountered no evidence of coercion by whites against blacks. The army officer even found himself popular, and was invited to go hunting with several leading citizens of the county.[58] Having removed most of the threats to success, certain Democratic leaders, who busied themselves campaigning, permitted the Independents and Republicans to hold meetings. One lady described a Bourbon political gathering held in October. Pleased by the oratory of the speakers, a judge from Selma and a lawyer from Demopolis, she wrote, "They showed conclusively the necessity of every white man casting his vote." She observed that "Six of the U.S. soldiers were in the audience, four all the time, and by their clapping" demonstrated that they were "of our sentiments." [59]

At the state level the Democrats carried the election. Taking advantage of Republican dissension, exploiting the economic crisis, resorting to irregular election practices when necessary, and most important, preaching the theme of white supremacy, the Bourbons ended Republican rule in Alabama. The campaign for the restoration of home rule was decided by an electoral verdict of 107,118 to 93,928. As exultant party newspapers put it, the state was "redeemed." [60]

In Choctaw County—despite everything that had hap-

58. Butler *Choctaw Herald,* February 24, 1875, quoting "Monmouth" in *Forest and Stream.*

59. Mrs. A. J. Ulmer to I. B. Ulmer, October 15, 1874 in Isaac Barton Ulmer Papers, Southern Historical Collection, University of North Carolina, Chapel Hill.

60. Going, *Bourbon Democracy in Alabama,* 26.

pened—the Bourbon Democrats won, but only by a narrow margin. In the governor's race Democratic candidate Houston defeated Lewis by a vote of 1,421 to 986, while Bailey was defeated for probate judge by only three votes.[61] What should have been an overwhelming victory by the Democrats fell far short. The explanation for the near debacle was that blacks, if not vocal during the campaign, were determined to vote; their determination sprang from the protective presence of the federal soldiers but no less from the work of Jack Turner, Edmond Turner, and Fred Barney who urged them to assert their political rights. The Republicans and Independents had done well, but the fact remained that the Democrats had won. "I have the honor to report," Lieutenant Egbert wrote, "that the elections on the 3rd instant passed off without disturbance of any kind having occurred." [62]

After the elections were out of the way, Jack Turner was brought to trial. Besides the charges of lynching and failure to answer an appearance bond, Jack had still another case against him. He and another black, Bill Burgess, who was also involved in the lynching charge, were accused of stealing ten dollars in greenbacks from a Negro named Jim Lassiter. No disposition was made at first (the case was not tried until 1875), but on November 9, the two men saw their indictments given by the grand jury to the circuit court.[63] On November 12, in the case of *State* v. *Jack Turner,* a terse decision was written

61. Official Returns, Governor's Contest, 1874; Butler *Choctaw Herald,* November 4, 1874.
62. Letter from Lt. Augustus R. Egbert (Microcopy 666, Roll 171, in National Archives Publications).
63. Grand Jury Docket, Book J, Fall Term, November 8, 1874, p. 11. See also Book P. Fall Term, September 23, Ooctober 8, 1874, p. 44, for *State* vs. *Jack Turner and Bill Burgess,* Circuit Clerk's Office.

into the case book: "state failed." The decision evidently
concerned some separate charge filed against Jack in the
Huff Cheney affair.[64]

On November 14 Jack Turner and the other men who
had held out for a jury trial pled guilty to the lynching
charge and were fined five hundred dollars. Apparently
they had decided or been advised that the guilty plea was
their best course. The same day the men faced, along
with Jack, charges of failure to answer an appearance
bond. Bond was set at one hundred dollars for each.
Several months later this charge was dropped against all
but Jack Turner who was tried but found not guilty.[65]
Since Jack could not pay his five-hundred-dollar fine he
remained in jail; he was anxious for release but unable to
secure it.

Having accomplished its mission, Company I was
ready to leave. Lieutenant Egbert received his orders on
November 19. If he had learned anything, it was to avoid
at all costs the discomforts of another march through the
wilderness of Choctaw County. Wisely he chose another
route: the men marched to the Tuscahoma Landing,
boarded a steamer for Demopolis, and from there took
a train to Atlanta. Leaving Butler on November 24, the
company reached Atlanta on November 28.[66] In a massive misstatement Lieutenant Egbert pronounced Choctaw County "perfectly orderly and law-abiding, and, after

64. Book P, Fall Term, November 12, 1874, p. 43, Circuit
Clerk's Office.
65. Book C, November 13, 1874, p. 309; Book C, May 3, 1875,
n.p., Circuit Clerk's Office.
66. Returns from Regular Army Infantry Regiments. See also
*Annual Report of the Secretary of War on the Operations of the
Department,* I (Washington, D.C., 1875), 52. See also Butler *Choctaw
Herald,* November 25, 1874.

diligent inquiry and examination I can see no prospect of change." [67]

In late November there was a rumor that Warner Bailey was preparing to bail Jack Turner "out of limbo." If the story proved true, the *Choctaw Herald* hoped "that Jack has learned a lesson this time which will operate as an effective reminder, in case he should again become possessed with radical devils." [68] The inmate was not so fortunate, for Bailey was unable to raise the money, and Jack spent the Christmas of 1874 in jail at Butler. In February, 1875, the jail lodged only two prisoners. "Jack Turner," the *Herald* remarked, "the concoctor and leader in the riot . . . last summer is one of the inmates. It is reported . . . that steps are being taken to turn him loose on the people again. It will be remembered that this Jack made his threats against every white man, woman and child between this place and Tuscahoma and [promised also to] give his old master five hundred lashes. Now after a lapse of a few months, his old master has loosened his purse strings and is ready to liberate him." [69]

B. L. Turner was among a small number of men who arranged for Jack's release in February. Within a few days misdemeanor charges were made against Jack, but no action was taken. At long last he was free to go home. The *Choctaw Herald* was furious. "Why should *he*," its angry editor asked, "for personal interest, be set at liberty on a bond, when the masses are in favor of his serving out his time in jail?" In fact, "for two or three men, backed by collaterals, to come forward and liberate such

67. Microcopy 666, Roll 171, National Archives Publications.
68. *Choctaw Herald*, November 25, 1874.
69. *Ibid.*, February 3, 1875.

a character as Jack Turner, is simply an outrage upon the good citizens of Choctaw county." [70]

Jack Turner had emerged in 1874 as a man of prominence in Choctaw County, no mean feat for a black man. In some mystical yet practical way—probably more felt than defined and certainly never reduced to a syllogism— he had known that political victory for his people might pave the way for economic triumph (or at least parity) as well and that the resulting benefits would aid him personally. He had shown qualities of natural leadership and examples of personal courage that inspired other blacks and caused whites to hate and fear, but also respect him. His political activities had marked him as an enemy to the Bourbons. More important, the "Invasion of Butler" had not only made him a fugitive; its implications, his detractors insisted, made him an enemy of the people. If future conditions warranted, Jack could be used as a bogeyman to fan the supposedly dormant fears of slave uprisings. The black man's pride was, if anything, greater than ever when the jail doors swung open in February, 1875. Had a detached observer been present, he might have suggested, and suggested correctly, that if Jack Turner had not heard the last of his foes, neither had they heard the last of him.

70. *Ibid.*

3

A Man of Worth

ATTEMPTING TO MAKE a living for himself and his family, Jack Turner faced the hard years of the seventies. The decade was one of economic depression that affected the entire country, but it hit especially hard in the South where recovery from the Civil War and the adjustment of Reconstruction were added burdens. The almost total lack of capital had a crippling, paralyzing effect on Alabama farmers and was given added poignancy when measured against the lives of black men. Jack and others like him had no industrial alternative to their struggle with the soil. For them the familiar tragedy and cruel workings of the crop lien and tenant farming systems became a burden and a curse.

Such was the milieu in which Jack Turner lived, and such was the system against which he fought. The Turner family eked out a hardscrabble living, acquiring even the most common household possessions gradually and painfully. Jack did not own personal property valuable enough to be taxed until the mid-seventies, and, of course, possession of the ultimate symbol of status, land

(cheap as it was), was a distant dream—but one not
forgotten.[1]

In 1877 Jack was saddened when he received news of
the death of B. L. Turner. The black man's former
master died at his Mount Sterling plantation on September 13, after suffering from paralysis for several months.
His death was briefly reported in the Butler *News.* Normally the death of a person of B. L.'s prominence would
have rated a eulogy of great length, but his Republican
ties precluded the testimonial.[2]

In drawing his will in 1875, B. L. Turner had specified
that he be buried in the family cemetery. Located near
his home, the burying ground was surrounded by a sturdy
iron fence. Jack Turner was selected to dig the grave for
the man who had been his friend and protector. Although
he would have gladly performed the service without com-
pensation, Jack was paid five dollars—B. L.'s family
made the gesture without condescension and Jack accepted the payment in the same spirit.[3] The planter-
businessman was buried beside his wife, Harriet King
Turner, who had died in 1865. (She was fifty-nine years
old at the time of her death, and B. L. died when he was
a few months past seventy.) Turner lay beneath an eight
foot column of granite topped by a right hand whose
finger pointed toward the open sky. The inscription read
"Rest In Heaven," and the grave's headstone recorded

---

1. The Assessment of Taxes on Real Estate and Personal Property records for Choctaw County, during these years has no record on
taxable property for Jack Turner.
2. Butler *News,* September 15, 1877.
3. Last Will and Testament of B. L. Turner, December 20, 1875,
Probate Judge's Office, Choctaw County Courthouse. See also Inventories, Choctaw County, Book C, 94, *ibid.*

the dates of his birth and death and the words "Our Brother." [4]

By 1878 Jack began to show marked economic improvement. As usual he paid his poll taxes, and there were also levies on his personal property—the total evaluation was a modest $42. Turner's "clocks and watches" were valued at $2, while his guns were worth an estimated $5. His most valuable possession was a $35 mule.[5] The next year Jack extended his farming operations. In February he received an advance of $110 in return for a lien on his crop, as well as additional security in the form of one gray horse and four milk cows.[6] His benefactor was Seth Smith Mellen, the remarkable principal of Mount Sterling Academy. Mellen was a native of Massachusetts who had taught in Georgia, Mississippi, and several counties in Alabama before coming to Choctaw County in 1869. With his fine head and black, slightly curly hair, Roman nose and face, and dark, expressive eyes, Mellen was every inch the patrician.[7] He sensed the strength and character of Jack and came to his aid. The loan was not the first, and it would not be the last time that Professor Mellen would render Jack an important service.

The black farmer negotiated two more loans in 1879.

4. The authors are indebted to the Rev. George Myers of Choctaw County who helped them locate the family burial ground. The iron fence stands today. Unfortunately some of the graves, including those of B. L. and his wife, have been desecrated.

5. Choctaw County Assessment of Taxes on Real Estate and Personal Property, 1878.

6. Choctaw County Record of Mortages, Book S, 483–484.

7. For information on Mellen see John Massey, *Reminiscences Giving Sketches of Scenes Through Which the Author Has Passed and Pen Portraits of People Who Have Modified His Life* (Nashville, 1916), 70; and DuBose, "History of Mount Sterling," 343–47.

A few more days after giving a lien to Mellen, Jack borrowed $35 from one Cyrus May. As security Jack offered Berry and Jonas, his yoke of oxen, and two wagons. In May he purchased supplies worth $23.83 from O. C. Ulmer and Company. He gave as collateral the same yoke of oxen and the same two wagons—fortunately, he was able to pay both Ulmer and May. The Negro also agreed, in case of default, to turn over to Ulmer a gray horse, four head of cattle, and twenty-five hogs.[8]

Although the late seventies were years of continuing trouble for Jack, they were also years of hope. He was a man of religious faith and was a member of St. John's Methodist church located near Mount Sterling. Jack also believed in hard work and made a solid beginning as a farmer. In 1876 Chloe bore him another son. The baby, whom they named Taylor, would be their last child.[9] As Jack became more important as a political leader, he saw the advantages of being well informed. In 1878 he astounded Editor William E. Beggs of the *Choctaw County News* when he and Richard Turner, another Negro, subscribed to the paper. By this time Jack had by diligent effort learned to write his name, but it is doubtful that his reading went beyond making out a few words. But he could have the paper read to him by his friend Fred Barney. Editor Beggs not only accepted his money, but congratulated him in print.[10]

Jack Turner's central role in the controversial "Invasion of Butler" in 1874 was reason enough for the county authorities to keep his activities under surveil-

8. Choctaw County Record of Mortgages, Book S, 523–24; Book T, 418–19.
9. Population Census for Choctaw County, 1880.
10. *Choctaw County News,* June 13, 1878.

lance. In the next few years the black faced a new parade
of charges. As the result of true bills being returned
against him, Jack went before the circuit court on two
successive days in the fall of 1875. In the first case, on
November 3, he and another black, Bill Burgess, were
finally tried—they had been indicted in the fall of 1874
—on a charge of having robbed Jim Lassiter, also a
Negro. The indictment was amended by the addition of
an assault and battery charge. Some kind of agreement
must have been reached because Jack pled guilty to the
second count. He was fined $250. The sum represented
such a stiff monetary penalty that a reconsideration was
made. A few days later the court, agreeing that the
amount was excessive, reduced the judgment to $150.[11]

The next day, November 4, Jack was in court once
again. He pled guilty along with Joe Turner, Ike Turner,
and Allen King to the offense of meeting together to
commit a breach of the peace. The wording of the charge
was inexact but all-encompassing, and the specific trans-
gression the men had in mind is not known. Following
their admission of guilt each of the Negroes was fined
$25.[12] In two days' time Jack had been fined a total of
$175, and he had to work long and hard to pay off his
sureties.

Sometime in 1877 Jack got involved with a Negro
woman named Eliza Moseley. Whether such activity outraged the moral sensibilities of the community or whether
Jack's adversaries saw an opportunity to discredit and
punish him cannot be documented. Yet it is a matter of

11. Choctaw County Circuit Court Records, Book C, 425, 449,
and Motion Docket, Fall Term, 1875, p. 62, Circuit Clerk's Office.
12. Choctaw County Circuit Court Records, Book C, 433. The
case may have had some tangential connection with the "Invasion of
Butler" charge.

record that Jack and Eliza were arrested and brought before the grand jury of the circuit court during its spring term. The grand jury had to decide if Jack and Eliza were in fact living together or if their intimacy consisted of single acts of illicit intercourse without any purpose to its continuation. The decision was to return a true bill against them with the charge that they "did live together in a state of adultery or fornication." [13]

Included in the evidence for the state was the testimony of J. B. Turner who had lived on the same place as Eliza Moseley for fourteen months. He swore that she was an immoral woman who had an infant seven months old. J. B. Turner said he had often seen Jack at Eliza's house at midnight and had seen him coming out at daybreak in his shirt-sleeves. He had also seen Jack playing with the child. Sam McVey told the grand jury that he had observed Jack at Eliza's house late at night and early in the morning and that her children called him papa. McVey swore to having seen Jack lie down on Eliza's bed in her presence, but admitted she had not been in the bed. Tucker Kemp testified that Jack was a frequent visitor at Eliza's, and Peter Foster declared that Jack told him he had whipped Eliza's husband for burning up a baby crib that he had given his mistress.[14]

The true bill was returned on May 4, and Jack and Eliza were tried before the fall term of the circuit court. They declared their innocence, but were found guilty. Each had to pay a fine of $100 and $36.90 in costs. Eliza was able to find sureties, and Jack turned once more to Professor Mellen for aid. The teacher, whose moral code was inflexible, did not hesitate to put up the

13. *Ibid.*, Book J, Spring Term, 1877, pp. 123–24.
14. Choctaw County Grand Jury Records, Spring Term, 1877.

money for the convicted man.[15] There is no way to be certain about the charges. Whatever Jack's relationship with Eliza was he continued to live with and support Chloe and his children—a fact the brilliant Mellen well knew.

After 1874 Jack increased his participation in politics —he had long since realized that political power was tied to economic power, and although there was never any hint that he desired economic or political dominance, he demanded and fought for equality in both spheres. Neither he nor his race was in a position to exert economic pressure, so politics remained the vehicle through which the desired ends might be achieved.

The dramatic election of 1874 had broken Republican control and returned the Democrats to power in Alabama. The Bourbons were scarcely ensconced before they set about undoing every vestige of Republican hegemony. Not the least of their acts was to draft a new and conservative state constitution that was duly ratified by the voters. The congressional districts were rearranged by a legislative act: Choctaw and Marengo counties were taken from the old Fourth District and made part of the First District. The scarcely concealed purpose was to break up the threat posed by the enclave of black counties. By balancing the two Black Belt counties with Clarke, Washington, Monroe, and Mobile, where there were many white voters, the chance of Republican success in congressional elections was greatly lessened.[16]

In the important gubernatorial election of August,

15. Minutes, Choctaw County Circuit Court, November 9, 1877, p. 125.
16. *Acts 1874–75*, p. 115. See also Malcolm Cook McMilan, *Constitutional Development in Alabama, 1798–1901* (Chapel Hill, 1955), 222.

1876, the Bourbons faced a test of power. Success in 1874, while seriously injuring their opposition, had not demolished it—if any reminder were needed, an embarrassing number of blacks still sat in the state legislature. Another triumph in 1876 was needed to make the Bourbon restoration permanent. Confident of victory, the Democrats nominated George S. Houston to succeed himself. The disorganized Republicans and Independents offered a coalition candidate: Noadiah Woodruff, a wealthy merchant and planter of Selma. The compromise "Independent State Ticket" stood little chance against Houston who swept to victory. Although the total vote was reduced from that of 1874, the margin of Democratic victory was much greater and indicated Democratic consolidation of power over Negro voters in the Black Belt.

The Montgomery *Advertiser* announced the returns from Choctaw County as 1,066 votes for Houston to 0 for Woodruff. The one-sided vote came because the Republicans and Independents were slow in organizing and failed to get out a ticket—their partisans simply had no one to vote for.[17] On the national level Rutherford B. Hayes of Ohio was nominated by the Republicans to succeed Grant, and the Democrats named Samuel J. Tilden of New York. The Independents and Republicans were better organized for the November election, but Tilden carried the state—including Choctaw County by a vote of 1,209 to 693—and the Democratic congressional nominee won in the First District.[18]

Although it seemed that Tilden had been comfort-

17. Montgomery *Advertiser*, November 19, 1876. See also Butler *News*, July 28, August 4, 11, 1876; and Going, *Bourbon Democracy in Alabama*, 50.

18. Butler *News*, November 16, 1876.

ably elected president, Hayes finally won the famous disputed election by being awarded the crucial electoral votes of Florida, South Carolina, and Louisiana. As president, he instituted a program designed to regain the South for the Republican party. The Republican president packed away the "bloody shirt," removed federal troops, and did not interfere with the restoration of home rule. Hayes appointed a Southerner to his cabinet, as well as Democrats and former Whigs to various offices, toured the former Confederacy personally, and advocated internal improvements designed to build up the South.[19] To a large degree Hayes abandoned the Negro, but even so, his program failed. His own party was split among warring factions, while most white Southerners remained loyal Democrats. Local and state interests, particularly maintaining white supremacy, were simply too strong.

In Choctaw County, Jack Turner and the blacks proved themselves practical politicians. They would have preferred a separate Republican ticket, but agreed with white party members that cooperation with the Greenbackers and Independents was necessary. There was no way to stop the election of Rufus W. Cobb for governor in 1878—Cobb was from Shelby County, had served in the Confederate army, and was a close advisor of Governor Houston.[20] Yet that fall white Republican leader

19. For the significance of the election and its aftermath see C. Vann Woodward, *Reunion and Reaction: The Compromise of 1877 and the End of Reconstruction* (Boston, 1951); Stanley P. Hirshon, *Farewell to the Bloody Shirt: Northern Republicans and the Southern Negro, 1877–1893* (Bloomington, 1962); and Vincent P. De Santis, *Republicans Face the Southern Question: The New Departure Years, 1877–1897* (Baltimore, 1959).

20. Butler *Choctaw County News*, August 1, 15, 1878. For Cobb's background see Owen, *History of Alabama and Dictionary of Alabama Biography,* III, 356–57.

Judge Luther R. Smith and blacks Jack Turner, Fred Barney, and others effected a coalition with the Greenbackers. Thomas H. Herndon had recovered from his defeat in the governor's contest of 1872 by serving as a member of the state constitutional convention of 1875 and as a member of the state House of Representatives in 1876–1877. As a resident of Mobile, Herndon had a formidable power base. He was nominated for Congress and carried the First District with a staggering majority of 3,636. But he lost one county: Choctaw. Herndon's scarcely known coalition opponent beat him 752 to 566.[21] Bourbons publicly dismissed their defeat as unimportant, an example of overconfidence, of letting down their guard. Privately they were not so sure.

Throughout 1879 Jack continued his farming operations, kept busy politically, and ignored the sniping of the local paper. Editor Beggs never ceased to be shocked at (or to report) the conduct of the man he derisively called "Captain Jack." No matter how it was intended, the use of the word *Captain* carried a measure of respect.[22]

By early 1880 the county's Greenbackers were well organized. Coming out of a series of secret meetings was the absorption of the Independents and the tacit promise of cooperation by the Republicans.[23] Jack Turner and other Republicans, mostly blacks, kept their organizational structure but decided that in the summer elections their best course was to support the Greenback candidates. The Greenbackers met in state convention at

21. Butler *Choctaw County News,* November 7, December 5, 1878.
22. *Ibid.,* August 7, 1879.
23. *Ibid.,* January 7, 1880.

Montgomery and nominated for governor the Reverend
J. M. Pickens of Lawrence County. There was little ex-
pectation that Pickens, whose home was in the Tennessee
Valley, would make much of a contest against Democratic incumbent Cobb. It would certainly be no race at
all in the Black Belt. Nevertheless, Jack Turner and other
blacks campaigned strenuously for Pickens. The Negro
leader became so active just prior to the election that
the newspaper in Butler issued a clear warning: " 'Captain Jack' had better go slow." [24]

In the statewide election on August 7, Cobb, as predicted, won a landslide victory, defeating Pickens
134,908 to 42,363, a margin of 92,545 votes. Cobb's
majorities in the Black Belt counties were crushing, but
in Choctaw County the efforts of Jack Turner and others
produced unexpected results. Although the surprised
Democrats won all of the races, each was closely contested, and while Cobb had a majority, his final total was
only 1,432 votes to Pickens' 1,132. [25]

The national elections in November promised to be
even more interesting. For president the Republicans
nominated James A. Garfield of Ohio, and the Democrats
countered with Winfield S. Hancock, a Pennsylvanian.
Temporarily abandoning Hayes's conciliatory Southern
policy, Garfield waved the bloody shirt. Once elected he
would move toward a different strategy. [26] James B.
Weaver of Iowa bore the standard for the Greenbackers.
There was little difference, save on the question of the

24. *Ibid.,* August 4, 1880.

25. Election Returns, Governor's Contest, 1880; Butler *Choctaw County News,* August 11, 1880; Going, *Bourbon Democracy,* 58.

26. See Vincent De Santis, "President Garfield and the Solid South," *North Carolina Historical Review,* XXVI (October, 1959), 442–65.

tariff, between the platforms of the major parties. The Greenbackers favored monetary inflation, of course, and other reforms such as a graduated income tax, woman suffrage, and federal regulation of interstate commerce.

Alabama's First District would participate in choosing a president, but it had sole responsibility for electing a congressman. With few dissenters, the Democrats renominated the venerable Herndon. Their narrow victory in August indicated to them that, among other things, Jack Turner was becoming an increasingly dangerous political adversary. Without doubt the Negro leader was convinced that the familiar harassment was beginning again when he was arrested in late September. He was accused of using profane language in the presenece of a female, but made bond and continued to take part in politics. Reduced to basics, the trial involved the word of his accuser against that of Jack. When the case came before the county court in October, he was found not guilty.[27]

In the First District, Republicans and Greenbackers were uncertain about a candidate, and their difficulties mounted. F. H. Threat (sometimes spelled Threet), a Negro Republican of Demopolis, was nominated for Congress by one convention. Another conclave repudiated the Marengo countian's nomination and endorsed James Gillette, a white Republican of Mobile. The mustachioed Gillette, a native of New York, had served as a major in the Civil War and been promoted for gallantry. He settled in Mobile after the conflict and held several positions, among them register in chancery and United States Supervisor of Elections for the First Dis-

27. Butler *Choctaw County News,* September 29, 1880; Special Citizens' Report.

trict.[28] Despite Threat's complaint that he was being discriminated against because he was a black, the truth was that the Republicans, seeking common cause with the Greenbackers, simply had difficulty deciding on a nominee. In any case, C. C. Pontiac, a white Republican from Mobile, and Jack Turner lent powerful campaign support to Gillette by making speeches in his behalf.[29] Although Threat refused to drop out of the race, he received only scattered support.

When the ballots were cast in November the nation, obviously weary of bloody-shirt tactics, gave Garfield only a narrow victory over Hancock. The Ohioan's popular margin was less than ten thousand in a turnout of more than nine million voters. Weaver ran a poor third, receiving less than half a million votes. Hancock managed to carry Alabama, but in Choctaw County the race was close. Garfield received 520 votes, Weaver 702 votes, and Hancock 1,050 votes. Democrats faced the disconcerting fact that had the Republicans and Greenbackers combined on a single candidate, Hancock would have been defeated. Choctaw countians demonstrated as much interest in the congressional race as in the presidential contest. Herndon received 1,076 votes to 16 for Threat and 791 for Gillette.[30] Although the final returns indicated a clear victory for Herndon, the Republicans charged fraud.

The November election had important repercussions

28. Butler *Choctaw County News,* December 3, 1881, quoting Mobile *Daily Register.* Gillette died in late 1881.

29. Butler *Choctaw County News,* November 3, 1880; Contested Election, *James Gillette* v. *Thomas H. Herndon,* House Miscellaneous Doc., 47th Cong. 1st Sess., v. 5, No. 16. For testimony of Threat, see 280–84.

30. Butler *Choctaw County News,* November 10, 1880.

for Jack Turner. He and his followers had the voters of Mount Sterling Precinct organized and ready. In fact, the precinct was the only one where Gillette gained a big victory, although in other of the county's precincts he barely lost. Mount Sterling voters preferred Gillette over Herndon 226 to 71.[31] Because the issue in his home precinct was not in doubt, Jack was free to concentrate on getting out the vote in the important precinct of Butler where the election might be lost or won. The voting place in the county seat was the courthouse. In conformity with election laws, there were inspectors and United States supervisors present to see that the voting was orderly and proper. Jesse Wilson, a Negro Republican and friend of Jack Turner (and destined to share an even closer relationship with the black man), represented the Republican party as a United States supervisor.[32]

Apparently it was Jack who devised the strategy of having himself and other blacks act as witnesses to insure further that voters would not be intimidated. Part of his plan involved having two men, Jerry Dick and George Wilson, keep a tally of the voters as they entered the courthouse. At one point the sheriff and the solicitor tried to disperse the Negro tally keepers, but Jack rushed to their defense asserting their right to keep a tally if they chose. The officials seized Turner and prepared to take him to jail. Thinking better of it—perhaps the knowledge that the election was a national one and any subsequent investigation would involve federal authorities influenced their reconsideration—they released him, and the tally went on. After the polls closed the ballots were counted and Gillette had a majority. But the count

31. *Gillette* v. *Herndon*, 108.
32. *Ibid.*, 150.

revealed that more votes had been cast than there were voters. After several recounts the returns were changed so that Herndon, not Gillette, had a substantial majority. An exasperated Jesse Wilson left after two hours, despite pleas by Jack Turner and several blacks to remain.[33]

In the rest of the state there were numerous election irregularities. In the Eighth District, Greenback Congressman William M. Lowe successfully contested the election of Democrat and Confederate hero General Joseph Wheeler. Republican James Q. Smith also won a contested election in the Fourth District.[34] A disappointed Gillette decided to contest. In his specifications Gillette charged illegal procedures in the Choctaw County precincts of DeSotoville, Butler, Isney, and Bladon Springs, and in other counties in the First District.[35] Jack Turner, a Negro named Ben Moss, and J. D. Flint, a white man, were summoned to Mobile as witnesses for Gillette. For some reason they never testified, although the possibility that Jack might give evidence caused one Bourbon to write, "Jack Turner will no doubt concoct a huge cock-and bull story to the effect that negroes were not allowed to vote." [36] Although he marshaled strong arguments and succeeded in getting

33. *Ibid.*

34. Frances Roberts, "William Manning Lowe and the Greenback Party in Alabama," *Alabama Review*, V (April, 1952), 100–21; and Going, *Bourbon Democracy*, 58; Chester H. Rowell, *A Historical and Legal Digest of All the Contested Election Cases in the House of Representatives of the United States from the First to the Fifty-Sixth Congress, 1789–1901*, 56th Cong., 2nd Sess., House Doc. 510 pp. 364–68.

35. *Gillette* v. *Herndon*, 3; Mobile *Daily Register,* December 18, 1880, January 23, 1881. Two other coalition candidates also contested but failed to unseat their Democratic opponents. See Rowell, *Contested Elections*, 362–64.

36. Butler *Choctaw County News,* January 19, 1881.

Herndon's majority reduced, the Republican candidate failed to unseat his opponent.

The elections of 1880 left a bitter aftertaste in the mouths of Choctaw County Democrats. Most of their displeasure was directed against Jack Turner. It was he, probably more than any one individual, who caused the near-defeat of the Democratic candidates for governor and Congress. Worse, he had been present at the polls urging black men to vote Republican, and defying county authorities, he had successfully opposed attempts to interfere with the Negro tally keepers.[37] The arrogant black had trod dangerous ground before, but this constant and unrelenting work in organizing the Negroes and persuading them to stand up for their rights had ceased to be a mere nuisance. If his efforts were successful, a return to the evils of Reconstruction was possible, or even worse, a profound reordering and restructuring of society might ensue. Shortly after the election, a choleric and threatening editorial appeared in the *Choctaw County News:* "Jack Turner and a few other tenth-rate local politicians, some of whom claim to be representatives of the Caucasian race, will have to be taught by some means or another, that they cannot run rough-shod over the white men of this county in their dishonest and revolutionary purpose of controlling our county affairs. If gentle means will not deter them, severer measures will be brought into requisition." [38]

The "Carnathan Affair" was another aspect of the politics of 1880 that deeply affected Jack Turner. If nothing else, the affair indicated what the "severer measures" hinted at in the *Choctaw County News* might

37. *Ibid.,* November 10, 1880.
38. *Ibid.*

mean and demonstrated Jack's influence with members of his race. Civil War veteran William G. Carnathan was one of the county's most prominent planters and a dedicated Democrat. His attitude, conditioned by his environment, was shared by a number of the whites in the county. The difference was that Carnathan was in a position of influence. Republicans charged that Carnathan forced his workers to vote Democratic. According to the allegations, Carnathan intimidated at least forty voters, and on the day of the November election stood at the polls for a considerable period threatening blacks who proposed to vote the Republican ticket. More specific accusations against him involved two black workers on his plantation, William Manning and Charley Dunn.

According to one story, on the day of the election Dunn accompanied Carnathan to Butler, but at some point eluded him, made his way to the polls, and voted Republican. Later, Carnathan found out about Dunn's flouting of orders, and the night after the election called his worker to task. Carnathan was alleged to have taken a bullwhip and severely beaten Dunn in the presence of the black's wife, William Manning, and others.[39]

A white Republican lawyer, George Turner (who had handled Gillette's contested election case and who was emerging as the leader of his party in Alabama), supplied one version of what happened to William Manning. As related by George Turner—who based his story on interviews with Manning and on testimony given before a federal grand jury and later before a United States circuit court—on November 2, Carnathan told Manning to hitch up the mules and get the other workers. They

39. See *Gillette* v. *Herndon*, 4, and 150 for statement of C. C. Pontiac.

were going in to vote. At that time Manning informed
Carnathan that he had voted as his employer had directed
in many elections, but that it had never done him or his
people any good. Manning then announced that he had
decided to stay at home and not vote at all. An angry
Carnathan had two men seize Manning, take him to the
barn, and tie him by his wrists. Carnathan then proceeded
to whip him with a heavy leather mule trace that had
an iron hitching hook on the end of it. George Turner
said that two months later Manning's back still had open,
running sores as a result of the whipping.[40]

Philip Joseph, black editor of the Mobile *Gazette,* denounced "such treatment of the colored people by the
few irreconcilable Bourbons." In Butler, Editor Beggs
denied any wrongdoing by Carnathan, declaring that,
in fact, more Bourbons were needed. "The growing evil
of the day is, that men who once made the negro know
his place and keep it, are fast losing their Bourbonism
and seem disposed to yield gradually to the darkey more
rights than he is entitled to." [41]

In the confused events that followed, proving the
time of the whippings was vital. There were several reports that Manning was beaten in August after the state
elections, while Dunn's whipping came after the national
elections in November. Since it would be Manning, acting on the advice of Jack Turner, who would press a
case against Carnathan for intimidation of a legal voter,
it had to be established that his flogging occurred in
November. Otherwise a United States court had no juris-

40. See interview with George Turner in New York *Times,*
August 26, 1882.
41. Butler *Choctaw County News,* February 2, 1881; see *ibid.,*
quoting Mobile *Gazette.*

diction; it could not hear a complaint arising from a state election. Dunn's misfortunes did not lend themselves to a federal case. He might be able to prove that he had been illegally beaten, but the event came after he had voted, not before. It would have been impossible to prove that Carnathan had prevented him from exercising his right of franchise.

Carnathan's defenders admitted that the black men had been chastised but insisted that the punishments had nothing to do with politics. The contention was that sometime in August, Carnathan had difficulty with Manning and "whipped him for personal insolence." As for Dunn, he too had been whipped, but it was in December not November and had nothing to do with any election, state or national. Dunn was punished "because he was suspected of stealing seed cotton, and resented reproach on the subject by drawing a knife." [42]

Although there was sharp disagreement over what had happened, Jack Turner was convinced that Manning had a legitimate case against Carnathan. He persuaded Manning to go to Mobile and testify before the grand jury of the circuit court, southern district of Alabama, during its December term. The term extended over into January, 1881, and it was in that month that Manning, Jack Turner, and other witnesses arrived. Charley Dunn was not present, although what had happened to him was related, including that he had been forced to hire out to Carnathan for another year. Manning's case was handled by United States Attorney George M. Duskin, who was assisted by George Turner. Their presentation was convincing, and the grand jury returned a true bill. The major charge was that Carnathan had prevented a quali-

42. Butler *Courier,* September 6, 1882.

fied voter in Choctaw County from casting his ballot for James Gillette. He had accomplished this "by assaulting the said William Manning with force and arms, and by then and there beating wounding and otherwise ill-treating the same William Manning to prevent him from casting his vote at said election." [43] Technically, it might have been argued that Manning's right not to vote had been violated, but in any event, Carnathan faced the humiliation of being indicted and bound over for trial.

The true bill was filed early in February, and a warrant was issued for Carnathan. The Choctaw County planter posted a five-hundred-dollar bond,[44] and awaited his trial which was set for the June term, 1881. A Butler editor claimed that none of the charges were true. They had been manufactured "by the Radical scoundrels who are the head and front of the political persecution" of Democrats.[45]

In March, after the litigants had returned home, the sheriff of Choctaw County placed William Manning under arrest. He was charged with hog stealing. An obviously pleased *Choctaw County News* asked its readers to note that this was the man who had testified against Carnathan. The obvious implication was that the testimony of a hog thief was open to serious question. What the paper did not discuss was that the charges against Manning had been preferred by Carnathan.[46] With all

43. Assession No. 54A308, Records Group 21, Federal Records Center, East Point, Ga. The true bill along with other related documents is filed in a packet.

44. *Ibid.*

45. Butler *Choctaw County News,* February 2, 1881.

46. March 30, 1871; Choctaw County Grand Jury Proceedings, Fall 1882, and Spring, 1883, p. 7, circuit clerk's office. The time sequence in the Grand Jury Proceedings "book" is confusing, but it seems evident that the events occurred as described. George Turner

of the complications in Choctaw County, it was not surprising that when the United States circuit court met at Mobile in June, the proper witnesses were not present. On motion of Carnathan's counsel, the case was continued to the December term.[47] The accused man's supporters reiterated their claims that the episode was a political plot by the Republican party, and objected to the expense and inconvenience Carnathan was suffering.[48]

Jack Turner, who was present at Mobile, pleaded with Manning not to give up. As George Turner described the situation, Jack was "looked upon as a representative and energetic colored man, [one] urging the prosecution of Carnathan, and preventing Manning from being either bull-dozed or coaxed into withdrawing or failing to press his complaint." [49] Before the case came up again certain developments affected the final outcome. Jack Turner had another set of encounters with the law.

If the Negro had forgotten that his conduct remained under close observation, he soon received an unpleasant reminder. In December, 1880, a resident of Mount Sterling held a sale, evidently at his home, and Jack was among those present. One of his critics wrote that "Jack Turner managed to raise another row. He left soon after the difficulty because discretion is the better part of

was in error when he said the charge against Manning was that of carrying a concealed weapon.

47. Minutes, Circuit Court of the United States, December, 1880, to October, 1884, Book D, RG 21, Federal Records Center, East Point, Ga.

48. Butler *Choctaw County News,* May 25, 1881. The paper's new editor was J. H. Stimpson who succeeded to the position after the death of Beggs.

49. Interview with George Turner in New York *Times,* August 26, 1882.

valor." [50] As always, the assumption was that whatever the difficulty, Jack was to blame.

But the black man was not allowed to get off so easily. Although the details are unclear, about the time of the sale he was accused of obtaining goods under false pretenses. The case came before the County Court and was nol-prossed on December 26. What happened in the courtroom is not known, but some remark, look, or gesture by Jack caused the judge to hold him in contempt and order him to jail.[51] Angry at what he considered the injustices of his confinement, especially on the day after Christmas, Jack retaliated by breaking out several window panes in his cell. As a result he was charged with "defacing" a public building and fined ten dollars. Although he could have put the money to better use, Jack had made his sentiments known, and since there was no real case against him, he was released on December 27.[52]

Jack must have reasoned that his political activity and his part in the Carnathan affair led to the attempt to resurrect the adultery charges against him. In the spring terms of 1880 and 1881, *State* v. *Eliza Moseley and Jack Turner* appeared on the circuit court's grand jury docket. In both instances Jim Lassiter, an old adversary, and Miranda Lassiter were the state's major witnesses, but despite their testimony the grand jury refused a true bill in either case.[53] It seemed clear that if Eliza had ever been Jack's mistress, she no longer was. The grand jury,

50. Butler *Choctaw County News,* December 22, 1880.
51. Butler *Courier,* October 21, 1882, citing Special Citizens' Report.
52. *Ibid.*
53. Grand Jury Docket, Choctaw County Circuit Court, Spring Term, 1879, to Fall Term, 1881, pp. 54, 96.

by its action, demonstrated an ability to carry out its functions with a sense of justice.

As for Manning, George Turner said that the worker was convicted and sentenced to hard labor for several months. He was later hired out by the state as a convict laborer in Choctaw County. In January, 1882, when the case against Carnathan finally came up, Manning's "custodian" permitted him to go to Mobile, and Carnathan paid his expenses. United States Attorney Duskin, George Tanner, and Jack Turner were astounded when Manning told them he was no longer certain that he had been whipped in November. It might have been in August. The lapse of memory, in the opinion of George Turner, came because he was influenced by fear and duress and possibly by reward. After all, Manning was serving a sentence and was present on sufferance from the planter to whom he was hired, and his expenses were underwritten by Carnathan.[54]

The prosecution's attorneys asked for a continuance in order that they might summon Charley Dunn and other witnesses who could establish the time of the whipping. The request was granted, and the trial was set for the June term, 1882. Supposedly, Manning reimbursed Carnathan as soon as his witness fees were paid by the court.[55]

Although they had won a delay, the government lawyers, as well as Jack Turner, recognized the inevitable. In June they tried but failed to obtain another continuance. Charley Dunn finally appeared as a witness, but

54. Interview with George Turner in New York *Times,* August 26, 1882.
55. Minutes, Circuit Court of the United States, December, 1880, to October, 1884, Book D, RG 21, p. 166.

his testimony was not needed. Choctaw County readers learned from their paper that Manning's "conscience got the better of his fears," and even though Jack Turner was not present to pressure him into lying, the Negro "swore it was in August not Nov. that he was whipped." [56] With such testimony from its star witness, there was little the prosecution could do, and Carnathan was found not guilty.[57]

Hatred of Jack Turner was no longer concealed in Choctaw County. It was not difficult to guess what Carnathan thought of him, and other citizens deeply resented a Negro's ability to inconvenience white people and have them hauled off to federal court in Mobile. Jack Turner's transgressions were difficult to overlook. He had succeeded in getting a powerful white man indicted if not convicted. And his political influence caused the Bourbons acute discomfort—they had come within a few votes of defeat. With no apparent strain Jack had survived attempts to silence him by putting him in jail. Something, a growing number of people believed, ought to be done.

Amid the excitement and drama of political turmoil and court cases, there remained the demands of making a living. In 1880 Jack's economic situation showed marked improvement. Making preparations for his crop, Jack went to O. C. Ulmer and Company in March to obtain supplies. As a security he gave a lien on his cotton crop as well as on a mule, an ox, a gray horse, seven head of cattle, and a wagon. In April he needed additional supplies and signed a note with the merchandising firm of Lake and Marshall for $125. He pledged his crop, a

56. Butler *Courier,* September 6, 1882.
57. Minutes, Circuit Court of the United States, December, 1880, to October, 1884, Book D, RG 21, p. 210.

brown mule named Lizzy, three cows and calves—Straw-berry, Peck, and Lon—a "dry" cow named Eliza (one wonders if she were named for Eliza Moseley, and if so, whether Jack or Chloe named her), and twenty head of hogs. For taxing purposes his personal property was assessed at $88, the highest valuation he ever had.[58] Also in 1880, Jack's sister Barbara (who does not seem to have been a slave of B. L. Turner in 1860) and her two-year-old daughter, Winnie Turner, moved in with Jack and Chloe. The twenty-two-year-old Barbara worked as a laborer. She and Winnie became two more people for whom Jack was responsible.[59]

Although he had done well in 1880, Jack's fortunes took a dramatic upsurge in 1881: he acquired eighty acres of land. His friend, Seth S. Mellen (recently removed to Tuscaloosa to become co-principal of a female academy), sold him the acreage. The rich land was located close to the Tombigbee River between Mount Sterling and Tusca-homa Landing. The educator was determined to help Jack, and settled on three hundred dollars as a fair price, making the payments as easy as possible. It is not certain where Jack borrowed the money, but he gained clear title by 1881. In a gesture combining familial loyalty and wisdom, Jack had the property deeded jointly to Chloe and to his children. If something happened to him, the Negro wanted his family to have clear and undisputed claim to the land.[60]

Jack was more prosperous than he had ever been. His

58. Choctaw County Record of Mortgages, Book U, 301; Book V, 668. Choctaw County Assessment of Taxes on Real Estate and Personal Property, 1880.
59. Population for Choctaw County, 1880, pp. 80, 83. No other mention of Barbara or of any other members of Jack's family has been found.
60. Choctaw County Deed Record, Book N, 716, Probate Judge's Office. The land was located in Section 25, Township 13, Range 2.

land, valued at $100, combined with his personal prop-
erty (including a fine mule named Ribbon worth $80),
placed him in an economic category considerably higher
than that of many whites and the vast majority of
blacks.[61] Most important of all, at long last he had
acquired a new status. He could with pride and satisfac-
tion savor the feeling of owning land. The soil on which
he lived was actually, legally his.

In the spring of 1881 Jack had no difficulty obtaining
an advance of $38.78 from his favorite commission
merchant, O. C. Ulmer and Company. The merchant
accepted as security certain personal property, including
Chloe's kitchen furniture, and a bale of cotton. Apparently the crop was good, for in 1882, Jack planned
his most ambitious planting. In January he contacted
C. C. McCall, a prominent farmer and Greenbacker, who
loaned him $255. In return the Negro put up his mule
Ribbon and his entire corn and cotton crop.[62] Despite
falling prices and rising costs, Jack Turner's agricultural
prospects were bright.

In 1882 Jack like other Choctaw countians, turned his
attention to politics. By that time (and in contrast to the
rest of the Black Belt) Choctaw County Republicans and
Greenbackers constituted a powerful coalition, and Jack
Turner looked forward to the governor's election in
August and the congressional race in November. After
President Garfield was assassinated in office, his succes-
sor, Chester A. Arthur, pushed forward a Southern political strategy begun under the slain president. Arthur
hoped to break the Solid South by extending Republican

61. Choctaw County Assessment of Taxes on Real Estate and
Personal Property, 1881.
62. Choctaw County Record of Mortgages, Book W, 345–46, 654.

aid and cooperation to various Independent and Green-back movements in the region.[63] What became national Republican policy in 1882 had been adapted and implemented by Choctaw County Republicans as early as 1878. More of the same was planned for the upcoming elections.

Meeting in Birmingham, a Greenback-Independent-Labor conference nominated James Lawrence Sheffield, a north Alabamian of Marshall County, for governor. The Republican state convention, acting on the advice of its white minority, endorsed certain of the Greenbacker demands and offered support to Sheffield.[64] In Choctaw County, Jack Turner and the Republicans supported Sheffield and other Greenbackers seeking local offices. Since Governor Cobb had served his alloted two terms, the Democrats turned to north Alabama and selected Edward A. O'Neal of Lauderdale County for governor.

As always, August was the month for politics. Choctaw County farmers had "laid by" their corn during the first week of July, and a few days later, having done all they knew to do, consigned the fate of their cotton crop to Providence. The long, hot days of August allowed the crops to mature. It was a time when the cotton bolls turned from green to speckled brown. People were not yet tired of watermelons and cantaloupes, although in August they welcomed the ripening of horse apples (and another variety that was firm and red), Leconte and Bartlett pears, and small, hard, tasty native peaches. In the corn patches the fodder and ears began to dry and turn brown, conjuring thoughts of fresh-ground meal for

63. See Vincent De Santis, "President Arthur and the Independent Movement in the South in 1882," *Journal of Southern History*, XIX (August, 1953), 346–63.
64. Going, *Bourbon Democracy in Alabama*, 59.

cornbread. It was a month for religious revivals, and no
small part of the evangelical fervor was applied to the
political crusades.

Although the Democrats attempted to brand the fusion
ticket as an incongruous monstrosity (how could high-
tariff Republicans make common cause with inflation-
minded Greenbackers?), the coalition forces worked
from the premise that adjustments could be made and all
else was secondary to the main goal of defeating the
Bourbons. Jack Turner worked as never before, urging
the blacks to go to the polls and seeking solidarity among
his people. His efforts, as well as those of other active
party members, paid off. In the state the Greenbackers
elected twenty-two members to the legislature, and Sheffield received 46,386 votes to 100,591 for O'Neal.[65] Most
of the coalition vote was in north Alabama, as O'Neil
piled up large majorities in the rest of the state. But not
in Choctaw County. The Bourbons were dumbfounded
when the county's voters endorsed Sheffield over O'Neal
by a vote of 1,075 to 991.[66] Choctaw County's Democratic power structure was shaken to its foundations.

65. *Ibid.*
66. Official Election Returns, Governor's Contest 1882. One
James *A.* Sheffield got a scattered 27 votes. The Butler *Courier,*
August 16, 1882, gave the fusion ticket 1,101 votes to 992 for the
Democrats. The coalition ticket also won the contest for the state
House of Representatives.

4

August 19

ONE CAN IMAGINE that Jack Turner took understandable pleasure in the results of the bitterly contested governor's race. He might also, had he chosen, have claimed much of the credit for Sheffield's victory over O'Neal. For a Black Belt county to cast a majority vote for a Greenback-Republican fusion candidate bordered on the miraculous. Victory was achieved because of the efforts of a small group of anti-Bourbon whites and a large number of blacks, normally Republican, who were willing to fuse with the Greenbackers in order to defeat the Democrats. Jack Turner had played a major role in organizing meetings, publicizing speaking engagements, cajoling hesitant blacks into political activity, and urging them not to be afraid to vote. The constant and successful theme of the black leader had been that the Democrats could be defeated.

Democratic politicians were pleased with O'Neal's easy statewide victory but disappointed with their loss in Choctaw County. After the August 12 election, politics would be interrupted only briefly because the November congressional elections were to follow, and few doubted that the fusion ticket, provided a suitable candidate could be found, would make a strong race. Still fewer doubted that Jack Turner, who had helped engineer victory in August, would take a leading part in the congressional canvass. Another loss of Choctaw County to the hated black leader—even if the Democratic candidate won in the First District, as he surely would with the Mobile urban vote—would be distasteful to most whites, unbearable to a few.

The usual course of politics—district meetings, extended sessions and debates over nominees—was interrupted on August 15. On that Tuesday morning Desotoville (a small village and voting precinct twelve miles northwest of Butler), Allen's Mill, and a church campground (both two miles north of Desotoville) emerged as the geographical setting for certain events that followed. Sometime between "daylight and sunrise" that morning, Herd Brown, a young white boy of twelve, the son of W. A. "Will" Brown, found lying in the public road, still damp with morning dew, a few steps in front of his father's gate a "bundle of papers." The package was tied at both ends with a strip of brown calico and appeared to have been accidentally lost. The lad picked the packet up, untied it partially, but then without reading the contents, carried the mysterious bundle to his father.[1] Will Brown looked through the parcel and found that it contained a number of garbled, painfully con-

1. Choctaw County Grand Jury Proceedings, Fall, 1882, and Spring, 1883, testimony of Herd Brown, 100, Circuit Clerk's Office; see also Special Citizen's Report. The Special Citizen's Committee was made up of George W. Taylor, solicitor, First Judicial Circuit; L. L. Belsher, county superintendent of education; John A. Harmon, sheriff; B. H. Warren, judge of probate; R. A. Moody, tax assessor; Joseph Brietling, county commissioner; J. C. Chapman, clerk, circuit court; and S. P. Smith, county treasurer.

structed reports, letters, and minutes. They were, however, clear enough, once he began reading, to cause the farmer to recoil in alarmed disbelief.[2] The quiet, nonpolitical farmer, who had voted the Greenback ticket in recent elections, knew something had to be done. He took the packet to Thomas W. Allen's mill. The miller also looked through the papers and agreed to take them to Edward McCall, recently elected as the fusion candidate to the state legislature and prominent in the Desotoville area. After surveying the parcel's contents, the legislator and Allen consulted with another Desotoville resident, C. C. McCall, also in politics and a presidential elector on the Greenback ticket in 1880. The political affiliations of the McCalls became important in later developments. Both McCalls agreed that the attention of Solicitor George W. Taylor was urgently required.[3]

By this time several hours had passed. The men settled affairs at home, saddled their horses, and, taking the bundle of papers with them, rode hard to Mount Sterling where Taylor lived. The solicitor was aroused at about ten o'clock that night by the McCalls banging at his door. Any annoyance he might have had at being disturbed vanished when he was shown the papers.[4] Equally upset, the solicitor helped arrange a secret meeting the next morning of a "few of the citizens of Mt. Sterling and Butler" at the county seat. Those attending were never

2. Special Citizens' Report.
3. Choctaw County Grand Jury Proceedings, Fall, 1882, and Spring, 1883, testimony of W. A. Brown, 100–101; testimony of Thomas W. Allen, 101 (Allen had also voted the Greenback ticket); testimony of Ed McCall, 102 (McCall also showed the papers to one G. C. Christopher).
4. *Ibid.,* testimony of Ed McCall, 102; testimony of C. C. McCall, 109.

named. The hastily assembled committee examined the scrawled reports and concluded that action was imperative. The package of letters revealed Jack Turner to be the head of a carefully planned conspiracy directed against the whites of Choctaw County. An affidavit was made and warrants issued by Probate Judge B. H. Warren. Sheriff John H. Harmon, supposedly acting on the experience of 1874 when there was "armed resistance to arrest," assembled a large posse and early on Thursday morning began executing the warrants.[5]

The parties "against whom the evidence of a conspiracy was most strong" lived at scattered places in the county, but by moving swiftly and early, Sheriff Harmon and his men made the arrests without violence or protest —except for Mose Turner who escaped (and was next heard from in Mobile).[6] The most important conspirator, the one who had to be captured, was Jack Turner. The arresting officers must have been nonplused at how easily their mission was accomplished.

Jesse Wilson, Fred D. Barney, Peter Hill, Range West, Willis Lyman, and Aaron Scott were soon under arrest. Three of the men—Aaron Scott, Range West, and Mose Turner—had at one time been tenant farmers for B. L. Turner.[7] When Willis Lyman, a minister, was informed that he was being taken into custody, he replied matter of factly that it was all right with him, it was not the first time he had been arrested.[8]

5. Special Citizens' Report.
6. *Ibid.* Mose Turner was not cited by name in the report, but he was the man mentioned.
7. Advances to tenants on crop of 1878, Estate of B. L. Turner, Probate Judge's Office.
8. Choctaw County Grand Jury Proceedings, Fall, 1882, and Spring, 1883, testimony of H. J. Gray, 100.

There were two accounts of Jack's capture. One that appeared in several newspapers recounted how H. L. Gaines led the posse to Jack's home before day only to discover that he had gone to the landing at Tuscahoma. In close pursuit, the search party found Jack. The black was described as "a sadly disappointed man" because he "had failed to catch the down boat a few minutes before she left the landing." The supposition was that he knew of the loss of the papers near Allen's Mill, although "There is nothing certain to indicate that he was endeavoring to escape the country." [9] Why a man of such supposed evil cunning as Jack Turner would attempt flight from a public landing where authorities would be sure to look for him was a point his captors seem to have overlooked.

Gaines offered his own version of the arrest. Someone had informed him that Jack was at the home of a man named Tabb. According to Gaines, he and his men saw Jack's mule (most probably Ribbon) hitched at Tabb's kitchen door. Members of the posse were stationed outside, and Gaines boldly entered the kitchen. He found the Negro calmly waiting. According to Gaines, Jack had been at Tabb's home for two hours in the hope of buying some whiskey. Cautioned that he was under arrest, Jack walked to the kitchen window and observed two armed men outside. Another member of the posse stood at the door. "[I] told him he was my prisoner. He said all right boss." [10] Members of the posse, who had good reason to expect a gun battle, found the peaceful arrest an anti-

9. New Orleans *Daily Picayune*, August 24, 1882 quoting Meridian (Miss.) *Mercury*, August 23, 1882.

10. Choctaw County Grand Jury Proceedings, Fall, 1882, and Spring, 1883, testimony of H. L. Gaines, 103; see also *ibid.*, testimony of C. C. McCall, 109.

climax. There is no evidence that Gaines ever speculated on why a man in flight for his life would delay escape for two hours in order to purchase liquor.

The seven Negroes were brought into Butler without ceremony and placed in jail. But news of the conspiracy and the arrests had already spread across much of the county. By midafternoon small knots of men began appearing in town, and by dusk a crowd of two to three hundred had converged on the jail. As the story of the plot passed through the crowd, unspoken anger turned to mutterings of the need for action, and soon there were open demands that Jack Turner should be hanged.[11]

What had happened? What kind of conspiracy was Jack leading? The incriminating papers seemed to speak for themselves. If the documents could be believed—and a large number of people never doubted them—Jack Turner was the leader of a conspiracy that dated back to 1878. He proposed to culminate the four-year plot with a bloodbath. Taking advantage of their unsuspecting victims who would be assembled at the campground near Desotoville, General Jack Turner, as he was called in the minutes, and his men would destroy the people while they were at worship. Similar uprisings in the county would be timed to coincide with the thrust against the campground and would begin on September 17. The blacks intended to massacre all of the white people in Choctaw County—men, women, and children.

Because the papers discovered by Will Brown's son were so important, a close reading of them is necessary and revealing. The documents were reprinted in part, and in several cases entirely, by various newspapers, although

11. Butler *Courier,* August 23, 1882. The Special Citizens' Report, declining to cite a number, called the assembly "quite a large crowd."

the original documents have been lost. They overlap, run together, and are ambiguous; no names were inserted except those for whom writs were sworn out:

Aug. the 5, 1882. Mt. Olive. Capt. Jack Turner meet at night on the 5 of Aug. with his club and Capt. turner made a noble Peach and said he want all to join in a war and said that he had made up a club of 285 he want more to join him and good many raly to him (here follows a list of names omitted as no proceedings against them have been taken) and the list was to go over to Desotoville Precinct For Capt Peter Hill as it is our last Round. Don by order of the meeting

CAPT. TURNER, Ch.
JESE WILSON, Clerk.

the officers meeting aug. the 6 1882 at Peter Hill and Gen. Turner Jack in the chair and the Gen. and Capt. Turner Moses said that he wanted all the Democratic negroes kill and it was agree to and Capt. Peter Hill said he want all the Cu Kluck negroes it was agree to and Gen. Jack Turner made a Peach on his war say Dear Friends in the year 1878 we made up this Club and now we have got strong in to it and let us be mens. I have run with the white mens untill I got all Their art. last fall you all send me to Mobile Powder and shots and we have 800 gun and now on the 17 night of Sept. let us rally to our Place and be mens indeed. Gen. in Chair

F. D. BARNEY, Clerk.

and by the 9 of aug. all Desotoville Paper must Com to the Gen. Clerk at Tuscahoma ala so the Book may be ready to meet all of our officer to be corrected if any to be   Good by

MR. JACK TURNER, Capt.
Tuscahoma, Ala.

Club meeting Held on the Camp Ground C. C.:
Aug. the 8 night in going the last round we got more

to join us (names omitted) and this is all that we can get and this make No 31 in Desotoville Pre. Dear Sir its is hard to write on our work For have to write almost in the Dark and when this get to our Des. Clerk hand he will put it on the Book right For his is a better writer.

and also say to Gen. J. Turner that he must excuse my hand write Fed Barney to correct it on his Book when he get his list and I have Ben on the Capt. Growns to-night as you told me and every thing is all right.

Aug, the 10 1882. We met in the meeting our last time and number up our mens and we are by this time 400 in number and we want to know how many you all have in Desotoville B. t. Gen. Jack turner, Capt. Moses turner, Lu. Rands West, Zenson Coleman, Capt. S. Scott Aaron.

FRED BARNEY

We met in the Club with Capt. Peter Hill in the chair to Deside on killing and we agre to kill one on E. McCall Place 3 on Ed Watkins Place one on Capt. McCall Place only 5 in this B. t. and also we will be all right on the 17 Sept. at night the meeting Demand Mr. (name omitted) to take this our Papers to Capt J Turner at Tuscahoma by Wenday night and tell him that we have Done we can do.

CAPT. PETER HILL, Chair.

Dear Gen. J. turner we are not forgot what you said to us in 1878 when we first meet we keep it in remember.

CAPTAIN PETER HILL,

(Here follows a list of names omitted). We have got more mens (another list of names) this is all we can get in this B. t.

this is to certify that we in Club have promes to Give Mr. Willis Lymon 50 cts Per Day to Cary our paper and Corlect members For Club. As he is working by the Day. This the only way we can up our Club. Done by order of the Club July 1882. Gen. Jack Turner, Chair, Capt. Moses Turner, Vice Capt Peter Hill Gard. F. D. Barney Clerk. In Desotoville Pree.

CAPT. JACK TURNER, Seal.

Mr. Capt Peter Hill Dear Sir Please send me those paper in. We want to get all the member name on one Book and Dear Sir you must see Willis Lymon and get his paper and M (name omitted) and get his we want them in brfore we Be betray. Please com Down Sunday and let us know how many you got.

GEN. JACK TURNER

DESOTOVILLE LIST NO. 2

Cared to (name omitted) by Aaron Scot and Rands Wes. Plesc Don losse it Don by order of the Club meeting in June 1882 Tuscahoma, ala the if this way are Messrs. Gen. Jack turner, Capt. Moses turner L. (name omitted) S. (name omitted) Sec. Capt. Peter Hill D. B. t. Sec Gen. (name omitted) and Dont let be like that war we had before. We will Given up this time till we will kill all the white Forks mens and women.

F. D. BARNEY, Clerk.

(List of names amounting to 22.)

I close say I s try and Could not get any more and our Clerk wrote so bad I could not read it all to the Peoples so I Den all Could Doe and so I went to the Camp Groun and found it all right.

READ THIS TO THEM

General Jack turner meet in the chair and Capt. Moses turner to propar a meeting of a club and Dear F Friends we are com again to the Sec. War For our benfit in Choctaw County Ala and we are be on hand From 1878 on tell now and also we are ready now For our war and we want every B. t. in the co county to be all right, and we only have 23 no. in your B. t. and we will say to you all that we expect to kill all of white mens and women and Baby, and you of the cold, in your B. t. may Look out and we want our Friend the Bare of this to let nobody no into this whil we have but 23 in your B. t. I think Desotoville B. t. is very a Bad place For Black people and we are going to have it to our hand before manny days and us look For our best way to Doe this thing. We Please that the 15 Day of Sept. will be the best while all the white will

be at Camp Meeting For we wil a shi time any way and
we have only 23 in your B. t. and on that Day we will let
you and have 35 of our mens and your all must whact for
selfs and we are all right Down here in our ports and be
shew to slay from Baby up to the oldes and have no man
on this list that will Betray us like Huff Chaney did and
dont take none of them Clu Kluck negro on your list for
we going to kill them too. Please read this to ever one
that join you and you must take sora, Paper along with
you to sign your members names on and on the 31 day of
July you must go op to the Camp Meeting place and Look
over the place that you may understand and I will taken
Butler and Capt. turner tak Mt. Sterling and we have 800
guns in readiness and I see all the Boys and their seems to
be all right and say the 15 that their are going to raly to
the Polls and also I find here bout Desotoville the the
colored Friend are all Pretty much all of them are on the
white Folks sid and it was hard to get these 23 up and
also I meet with Mr. —— at the Camp Grounds night and
I Look over the Paper and could read good and also when
you take this off to rewrite in the record Please have a
good writer so that we can make out his hand write I
Learned that you are going to slay From the baby up to
the oldes and also you must Doe all you can in Butler
that Day for it will be a good time

F D BARNEY Clerk.

This our last meeting this sid of our time and we only
have 23 members in desotoville Precinct and we are
going take this County by Shedding Blood and we are
going to slay from the young up to the oldes and Capt
Jack turner is going with his mens that night to Butler and
Capt Moses turner will go up to the Camp Groun and Capt
Peter Hill will take his mens to the Mt. Sterling and
you must all Look out and be taking and we will meet on
the 17 night Sept For this will be our time when every
Body will have Preaching in minds Mr. Turner is our Gen
and when we take this County we will pay him Mr. F. F
Barney is our Book Keeper and we will pay him too.[12]

12.   Butler *Courier*, August 23, 1882.

Word of the sensational documents had spread rapidly through Butler and Mount Sterling, Bladon Springs and Pushmataha. Even while the angry citizens converged on the jail the damning packet was the subject of conversation in remote crossroads hamlets as men and women prepared to go to bed—for once crops and the weather were not the principal topic of conversation. A number of men in the crowd at Butler insisted that Jack Turner be hanged that night. But others, either a majority or men of greater influence, persuaded the crowd to move to the courthouse square. To the degree that discussion was possible, there was dialogue, although the *Courier*'s statement that the throng engaged in "mature deliberation" seems ludicrous. But on Thursday night the crowd was too shocked to rise to the frenzy of mob action. The proper backlash required more time, shock waves were still spreading, resentment still festering. Somehow the people agreed to postpone action until Saturday. It was agreed that on that day, August 19, a mass meeting of the county—whites and blacks—would assemble in Butler and decide what should be done.[13] Oak trees on the square had long since shut out the fading shafts of sun, and darkness fell on the town as the crowd dispersed.

The prisoners were well aware of what might happen to them. Chloe and the children learned of Jack's arrest but did not see him. They waited. Jesse Wilson, Range West, Fred Barney, Peter Hill, Willis Lyman, and Aaron Scott contemplated the next hours with dread and mounting apprehension. The highly intelligent Fred Barney must have envied Mose Turner, who had escaped, evidently with the aid or at least the approval of federal authorities. He was in Mobile under arrest for having vio-

13. *Ibid.* See also Special Citizens' Report.

lated federal timber laws. So long as he was a federal prisoner, Mose Turner was safe from prosecution by state officials. The latter were furious at being outwitted legally, but there was little they could do. All of the men arrested had been workers with Jack Turner in achieving the victory in August, all were active in the Republican party. Now they were in jail, hauled rudely in by a posse and confronted with charges of plotting an unthinkable crime. What would happen to them was beyond the prisoners' ability to know or control.

The men responsible for the arrests moved swiftly to punish Jack Turner, to eliminate him as a political threat and as a living, personal refutation to the carefully structured theory of white supremacy. Yet their actions went beyond all of this and exceeded the simplistic hate of a few whites for a black man. That the sequence of events was even *possible* was part of a time, place, and people. But whatever Jack Turner's enemies were, they were not philosophers. They were practical men. To be successful, their actions had to maintain a façade of democratic fairness. Even if unlawful extremities were adopted, what happened had to appear as the will of the people. Certainly the action of a people "performing in their majesty" could not afford the charge that some of the body politic had been drunk. To avoid such allegations, the owners of the Morning Call Saloon, the Exchange Saloon, and all other drinking establishments were compelled to close their doors.[14] There would be no whiskey evident when the Choctaw countians came into Butler on Saturday.

What would the sovereign people decide? They would examine, or hear read, the evidence. But would the al-

14. Butler *Courier,* August 30, 1882, mentioned that the barrooms were not permitted to reopen until Saturday afternoon.

leged letters and reports of General Jack Turner and his
men cause a reaction? Obviously they would, but what
kind of reaction? The assemblage might ask that the so-
called conspirators be freed, or jury trials might be demanded. Either course was possible if the crowd had no
more to base its action on than a parcel of letters found
on a country road near Desotoville. They needed an admission of guilt by one or more of the conspirators, and
the attempt to secure confessions began on Friday, August 18.

The arrested men strongly denied the conspiracy
charges. It was, of course, true that they were black, that
they had worked against the Democrats, but their opposition had been political, not racial or physical. They
had never, they argued, plotted to destroy the white people of Choctaw County. In selecting a conspirator likely
to confess, the men who wished to strengthen their case
did not choose Jack Turner. There was no need to attempt to coerce him. He could not be forced to utter a
word of incrimination against himself or the others. But
perhaps one or more of the remaining prisoners were less
resolute. If the fear that accompanied the fact of incar-
ceration was insufficient to force an admission of guilt,
the crude but effective use of torture was called for. A
Democratic newspaper admitted that "Jack's captains
were more or less scourged. One was treated to the in-
dignity of being tied up by a big toe and terribly tortured.
Still he refused to 'squeal.' " [15]

The man who maintained his innocence despite the
pain was Fred Barney. His inner strength prevailed, and
he "denied all knowledge of the conspiracy and affirmed

15. New Orleans *Daily Picayune,* August 24, 1882 quoting Meridian *Mercury,* August 23, 1882.

with Christian-like sincerity his innocence." [16] It was not possible that Barney could have been "borrowed" from the jail without the knowledge of the county officials. In a monumental breach of security, Barney was taken from the jail to a clump of woods half a mile distant. He later told a grand jury that he was first whipped with switches. "I was hung up by the neck to a tree until I was unconscious. I was frightened when they took me out. All of the men were strangers to me. Some one stuck me with a knife while they hung me up by the toes." [17]

Why did Fred Barney refuse to confess? A Democratic newspaper believed it was because "They all prefer death to giving up the secret it is morally certain they carry with them." [18] The New York *Times* countered that the "torture of 'JACK's captains' failed of its object, because the poor wretches had nothing to tell." [19]

Next the minister Willis Lyman was brought out. He too denied complicity. Lyman "knew nothing at first," one report explained, adding "but under the refreshing and persuasive influence of the lash, applied vigorously to his bare back, he remembered a great many things." [20] Lyman described the incident to a grand jury. A group of more than five men took him to the woods—presumably the same spot where Barney was tortured. The black was tied and part of his clothing removed. He was whipped with switches on his body and also on the tops and bot-

16. New Orleans *Times-Democrat,* August 22, 1882, quoting a story filed from Meridian, August 21.
17. Choctaw County Grand Jury Proceedings, Fall, 1882, and Spring, 1883, p. 38.
18. New Orleans *Daily Picayune,* August 24, 1882, quoting Meridian *Mercury,* August 23, 1882.
19. New York *Times,* August 28, 1882.
20. New Orleans *Times-Democrat,* August 22, 1882.

toms of his feet. A rope was put around his neck and he
was hanged until he lost consciousness. Recognizing two
of the men, Lyman identified them as Thomas A. Hightower and Thomas S. Addison. According to Lyman,
Addison helped tie him up, but the Negro did not know
if he participated in the torture. Hightower took part in
the whipping. "Mr. Hightower said he was going to make
me tell the truth or kill me. I was badly scared." [21]

Yes, the black sobbed, there had been a plot. Yes, Jack
Turner was the leader. The Negro explained that he had
been the custodian of the books and papers of the secret
organization and that he was paid fifty cents a day to re-
cruit new members. Ostensibly, he moved around as a
farm laborer working for fifty cents a day for white farmers. He had lost the papers by accident when on his last
recruiting round. Since the accounts spanned such a brief
time, were there not other reports and records of Jack
Turner's army? The suffering Negro said that there were
other records. In fact, after the arrests one of the blacks
asked Jack if the whites had found the remaining books.
Jack Turner replied, "No; they are not quite that d[amned]
smart." Despite Lyman's statements, additional whipping
failed to exact from him the whereabouts of the other
minutes.[22] Perhaps only Jack Turner knew where they
were secreted, but if Willis Lyman casually carried some
of them around, it would seem that he would have known
where the others were, and since he had already confessed, the minister would not have refused to reveal their
location and invite the additional torture that he received.

21. Choctaw County Grand Jury Proceedings, Fall, 1882, and
Spring, 1883, p. 37.
22. New Orleans *Times-Democrat,* August 22, 1882.

It appears certain that there were no additional documents; the black had been tortured into a confession, one that could be used as additional ammunition.

In considering the events that followed, it is important to realize that the fear that black chattels might rise in insurrection was as prevalent as it had been during the antebellum period and made the citizens susceptible to unscrupulous exploitation.

Early Saturday morning people started arriving in Butler. They came on foot, horseback, in oxcarts, and all manner of wagons and carriages. Almost one thousand people, over two hundred of them blacks, appeared. Women stayed at home, pulling the shutters to, closing curtains, lowering shades. Their mystified children begged to go out and play, wondering why they had to remain inside. In town the usual Saturday sounds—the cacophony of conversation, the jocular greetings, the proffered trades, and shrewd bargaining—all these commonplaces were missing. Instead the crowd moved without any direct orders but with unerring aim on the courthouse square.[23]

Once gathered, the crowd was organized into a public meeting to consider the situation. A chairman and secretary were chosen—their names were never revealed. As one newspaper explained, "Technically, it was a mob, but in reality, a committee of safety of the whole people." [24] The debate began sometime between ten and eleven in the morning and continued for two hours. Arguments

23. The description of Butler on this day is based on printed sources and interviews with people in Choctaw County who recalled stories related to them. Especially helpful were the recollections of Mrs. Arthur C. (Mattie Jo) Glover.

24. New Orleans *Daily Picayune*, August 24, 1882, quoting Meridian *Mercury*. See WPA MSS for the undocumented claim that Captain A. J. Gray was elected chairman.

pro and con were delivered, although contributions by blacks, if any, to the presentation went unreported and unrecorded.

Solicitor George W. Taylor and others wanted to compare the handwriting that appeared on the documents with that of the prisoners, including Jack. At best Jack Turner's writing ability did not include the skill, no matter how rudimentary, of recording the minutes of a meeting. As "general" such responsibilities would not have been his function in any case. Any arguments that he had written them were baseless. Those parts of the documents ascribed to Fred Barney would have been an insult to his intelligence, let alone his knowledge of spelling and grammar. The solicitor was on sound logical ground in his request. He suggested the appointment of a committee of eleven to investigate and compare the handwriting and report to the meeting. The chairman put Solicitor Taylor's question before the crowd, but it was defeated by a vote of 368 to 217.[25]

In the moments that followed the announcement of the vote, the sweat-soaked crowd realized the alternative and stirred in uneasy silence. Only one thing remained to be done. A motion to hang Jack Turner rose from the crowd, cut clearly through the heavy heat, and carried to the chairman for action. A journalist would explain later that "in this country when, in extraordinary emergencies, a committee of safety of the whole people is organized, all laws, for the time are in abeyance, and all constituted authorities. The great people in their primitive might and majesty are ruling." [26]

25. Butler *Courier*, August 30, 1882; New York *Tribune*, August 30, 1882, quoting a telegram from Washington D.C., dated August 29.
26. New Orleans *Daily Picayune*, August 24, 1882, quoting Meridian *Mercury*.

Whatever his own thoughts, the presiding officer performed the function for which he had been selected: for the second time that day the chairman put a motion before the people. The question was whether Jack should hang, and this time the vote was overwhelming. The Butler *Courier* placed it as 998 to 2.[27]

The chairman declared that Jack had been found guilty, and pronounced the death sentence. A committee of twenty-four was appointed to execute the verdict.[28] Jack Turner and the other men heard the sound of a brief scuffle at the front of the jail. It was now a few minutes before one o'clock. Members of the committee had appeared before Sheriff Harmon, demanded his keys, and when he refused, had taken them away.[29]

Probably from the moment of his arrest Jack Turner sensed that he would never return to Tuscahoma alive. Against odds impossible to calculate he had, so far, held his own, but now the bitterness and hatred that he had faced for years had accumulated and he was lost. With little doubt, images swarmed through his mind, and emotions coursed wildly and without order—but one emotion evidently took charge: unflinching bravery. Jack Turner accepted the final truth that he was going to die.

The six other prisoners watched in helpless awe as Jack was taken by the mob. He was described to have moved with quiet, unbowed dignity from the jail, and flanked on either side by his escorts, he proceeded to the courthouse square. His judges gave way as he walked past them, finally stopping before a large oak. Beneath its

27. Butler *Courier,* August 30, 1882.
28. Special Citizens' Report; New Orleans *Daily Picayune,* August 24, 1882, quoting Meridian *Mercury.*
29. Butler *Courier,* September 6, 1882; *ibid.,* quoting Mobile *Gazette.*

dappled shade stood a buggy. Jack watched with detachment as three men climbed the tree and tied a rope to a sturdy limb, and tended to other details of the hanging.[30] Would the condemned man like to speak? Did he have any last requests? Yes. He had two last requests. He wanted Chloe to come to him so that he might kiss her for the last time. And after the mob was through with him he wanted to have his body decently buried at Mount Sterling. As for Jack's speech, his delivery was described as steady, deliberate, unimpassioned. Simply and eloquently he declared his innocence.[31]

Chloe could not be found. It is possible that she was present but more probable that she remained at home with the children. After a brief and unsuccessful search for Chloe, the committee of twenty-four proceeded with its work. Jack was made to mount the buggy. A chair had been placed in the vehicle to provide the regulation fall, and Jack was directed to stand on the chair. His feet were lashed together, his hands were tied behind him, and finally the hangman's noose was adjusted. Did the condemned man want someone to say a prayer? No, he would pray for himself. Jack's prayer was the hope that God would receive his soul into heaven.[32]

It was now fifteen minutes after one. Suddenly the buggy moved forward. Jack dropped several feet, and the audience gasped as the rope snapped taut on the tree. His weight and physique were so great that the limb sagged and his feet touched the ground. Hurriedly several of

30. New Orleans *Daily Picayune*, August 24, 1882, quoting Meridian *Mercury*.
31. *Ibid.* See also Special Citizens' Report; New Orleans *Times-Democrat*, August 22, 1822.
32. New Orleans *Daily Picayune*, August 24, 1882, quoting Meridian *Mercury*.

Jack's executioners climbed the oak and untied the rope while others tugged on it to raise the limp, dangling man enough for his body to swing. After eight and a half minutes the rope was cut.[33] "He met his death cooly [*sic*]," an editor who hated Jack Turner admitted. The journalist wondered why he "died persisting in a stubborn denial of the charges contained in the papers." [34]

A number of people in the mob turned their heads and hurried away. Others came forward for a closer inspection. Some of Jack's friends got word to Chloe of what had happened, and she would come later to claim the body of her husband. For the moment the lifeless form of Jack Turner lay in the dust.

One editor commented, "And thus died one of the worst of his race that ever lived in Choctaw county—a bold, bad man, too dangerous to be let live a day longer." In fact, "The moderation of the citizens of Choctaw, under the circumstances, is a marvel and above all praise. We congratulate them upon their escape from a great and bloody danger, and hope now they can breathe freer and easier." [35]

33. *Ibid.* See also "G" writing to Montgomery *Advertiser,* August 23, 1882. "G" witnessed the hanging and filed his story that afternoon.

34. Butler *Courier,* August 23, 1882.

35. New Orleans *Daily Picayune,* August 24, 1882, quoting Meridian *Mercury.*

5
The Reaction

A FEW HOURS AFTER Jack Turner's body was cut down, two white men who had witnessed the hanging made a somber journey to their country homes. Hardly bothering to watch the stars come out, the emotionally exhausted farmers paused briefly at an acquaintance's house —perhaps to get a drink of water from his well. Anxious for news, their host (a white Republican who had remained at home during the day) was shocked and dismayed when he learned how Jack had died. There was no need to elaborate, and the men, after exchanging muted farewells, rode on.

In despair and rage, the Republican went inside and quickly scrawled a letter. Hoping somehow to ease his fury and frustration, the writer addressed himself to a political friend in Washington. "They still have Jesse and several others," he wrote. "Is it not terrible? No possible chance for [Jack Turner's] life; they only arrested him on Thursday, and tonight Saturday, he lies a corpse. I did not think they dared go to such an extreme, but now I sincerely believe it is not safe for a Republican to live among them, for now what can be done?" Very little, he

was convinced. "If it was a few men there could be a
chance to investigate the matter and bring the guilty to
justice, but it is the whole country now, and God only
knows what will become of it. Well, I feel like one alone,
for I do not believe there is even one that I could believe
a true friend." [1]

Saturday night could have been no less than a night-
mare to Jesse Wilson, Range West, Fred Barney, Peter
Hill, Willis Lyman, and Aaron Scott. They knew that
Jack was dead, and it seemed likely that a similar fate lay
in store for them. But nothing happened: Sunday came
and brought with it a drained sense of calm. The people
of Butler, whites and blacks, put on their stiffly starched
Sabbath clothes and went to church. It seemed possible
to the prisoners that the hangman's rope had been meant
only for Jack Turner. But it seemed certain that they
would have to stand trial. The men had been arrested on
conspiracy charges, an offense against the state designated as a misdemeanor and punishable by a fine of
$1,000 and six months in prison. In fact, the relatively
light sentence—even if conviction were achieved—had
been used to urge the mob to sterner action (and would
be used later to help explain the lynching). One angry
writer pointed out that the people had "risen above the
law and attached a punishment to a crime which even
the criminal code, hard as it is, treats with far more
moderation." [2] But the unctuous Butler *Courier* replied,
"The mighty and just indignation of an outraged people
appreciating the insufficiency of the penalty meeted [*sic*]
out for such crimes, took the law in their own hands and

1. Quoted in New York *Tribune*, August 30, 1882.
2. Camden *News and Pacificator,* October 6, 1882, quoting
Eutaw *Mirror.*

Jack Turner sleeps the everlasting sleep, and will never again ruffle the current of this people's happiness." [3] Fred Barney and the others debated whether to go before the county court and accept the verdict of the judge or ask for a trial by jury.

On Monday, August 21, the six men were taken out of jail and brought before the County Court. They pled innocent, and, carrying out a previously made decision, demanded a jury trial. The request was granted. After their bonds were fixed at one thousand dollars each, the accused returned to jail hopeful but not convinced that their cause would ever be heard. Their uncertainty was understandable in light of an editorial in the local paper: "Should they live to be tried the verdict of the jury will as certainly condemn them as the crowd did Jack Turner. The evidence is too strong to admit of any other result." [4]

In the silent hours after the hanging the grief-stricken Chloe and Barbara, Jack's sister, had gone through the numb motions of arranging for the body to be taken home. The young Turner children—Nelly, Beloved, Luther, and Taylor—were informed of their father's death. It can be imagined that despite her anguish and sorrow, Chloe told the children they should be proud of their father, proud of the man he was and of what he lived for and believed in. Within the next day or so Jack Turner's funeral was held. He was buried with simple ceremonies in the sun-parched graveyard of St. John's Methodist Church. Located immediately west of the church building, the cemetery sprawled without design or apparent boundaries. A few of the graves had granite markers, but more were graced by crudely lettered wooden plaques

3. Butler *Courier*, August 23, 1882.
4. *Ibid.*, August 30, 1882.

—even the most recent already decaying, while others stood or leaned at awkward angles, their imprinted records of birth and death long since faded and gone. Irregular mounds—some covered with fresh clay drying into brittle clods of earth, others, older, less raw, had runners of grass providing partial cover—with no markers at all indicated the final resting places for many.

Chloe did not have enough money to afford a granite headstone for her husband. A simple, wooden marker was probably put in place, but it would be lost with the passage of time. According to a local legend, impossible to document, Chloe, desiring to provide some kind of permanent commemoration, planted a small water oak at the head of Jack's grave. The tree, if it did not perish, would become a living marker. Whether the story is true or not, a massive, impressively beautiful water oak now dominates the Negro graveyard, giving it silent shade and enduring serenity.[5]

Because Butler was so isolated—there was no railroad, and the nearest telegraph was thirty-eight miles away at York in Sumter County—news of the hanging was slow in reaching the rest of the state and country. The first account of the lynching appeared in the Mobile *Daily Register* on August 21. Under a headline proclaiming A DIABOLICAL SCHEME, the story reached the *Register* in the form of "A letter from a trustworthy gentleman of Choctaw County." The correspondent's name was never known. His story was picked up by the Associated Press, sent out across the country, and became the standard account of the event. The gist of the brief dispatch was that

5. Authors' interview with Mrs. Charley Turner of Mount Sterling.

a conspiracy had been discovered, arrests had been made, Turner had been hanged, and all was quiet.[6]

Although a number of major regional newspapers did nothing but print the Associated Press story, the headlines they used were significant. In Tennessee what was proclaimed A CONSPIRACY by the Nashville *Daily American* became A FEARFUL CONSPIRACY to the Raleigh *News and Observer* in North Carolina. Kentucky readers were informed by the Louisville *Courier-Journal* of the fate of THE CONSPIRATORS, and in Little Rock the *Daily Arkansas Gazette* described their activities as A DARK PLOT. The affair had been A BLACK PLOT to the New Orleans *Daily Picayune* and A TERRIBLE REVELATION to the Washington *Post*.[7] None of these papers offered any editorial comment.

Surprisingly subdued were the headlines: A SENSATIONAL STORY, offered by the Charleston *News and Courier,* and A PROJECTED RIOT, reported by the Atlanta *Constitution*. A few days later the South Carolina paper, fearing an attack on the whites, hoped there was "not much hard fact in the story of the insurrection in Choctaw County, Ala., outside of the hanging of a negro." [8] The *Weekly Clarion* of Jackson, Mississippi, reduced the Associated Press story to a succinct three-sentence para-

6. See Hartford *Courant,* August 26, 1882, for sharp criticism of the Mobile *Daily Register's* failure to reveal the correspondent's name.

7. All of the headlines appeared in the August 22, 1882, issues of the papers cited. Alabama journals that carried the AP story included Birmingham *Iron Age,* August 24, 1882; Uniontown *Press,* August 26, 1882; Carrollton *West Alabamian,* August 30, 1882; Greensboro *Alabama Beacon,* August 25, 1882.

8. Charleston *News and Courier,* August 25, 1882, and for the headlines, *ibid.,* August 22, 1882; and Atlanta *Constitution,* August 22, 1882.

graph on the editorial page. In tone the editorial was in sympathy with the action taken by the whites, but there was no expression of total outrage, no horrified recounting of black treachery.[9]

The stark fact that Jack Turner had been hanged provoked a complex set of reactions: troubled, ambivalent, profound, tragic, and compelling. They took the form of the spoken word (and the unspoken word) and the written word. Political repercussions were not the least important of the events that followed the hanging. How could the murder be justified? If it could be, did the justification apply only in this instance and at this time, or was there a special category of crime that not only excused lynch law but made it necessary? If the hanging could not be dignified as essential for the preservation of some high principle, then how might it at least be explained, how could it be made acceptable? A rational analysis of *why* the crime was committed could (or might) erase part of the stigma that accompanied the deed. But what if all explanations were rejected? What if no amount of soul searching could eradicate the irreversible and bloody fact that a mob had gone beyond the law and taken a human life? If this proved to be the case, then there was no way to avoid the searing and painful process of admission of guilt. To their credit a number of Alabama and Southern newspapers (albeit a minority) as well as public officials and private citizens were willing to accept the burden and the blame and to place responsibility where it lay.

Not unexpectedly a number of Northern newspapers condemned the act as a savage violation of the laws of

9. Jackson (Miss.) *Weekly Clarion*, August 23, 1882. Similarly restrained was the headline "A NEGRO CONSPIRACY IN ALABAMA DISCOVERED," appearing in the Macon (Ga.) *Telegram and Messenger*, August 22, 1882.

humanity (they also, no less than partisan Southern journals, inserted politics into the issue). The outlets of expression for the blacks were extremely limited, but they did exist. Two Negro newspapers, the Mobile *Gazette* and the Huntsville *Gazette,* were outspoken in their denunciation of the mob. The editors of the black papers were angry and hurt by the act because it was both an assault on a man and his right to life and an undeserved and humiliating attack on their race.

No simple, uninvolved explanation could account for the lynching. The crime had dimensions both defined and undefined: the passage of years and events in which Jack Turner had, in the opinion of his adversaries, with impunity defied white society; the feelings of bitterness and frustration accompanying military defeat and grown deeper during Reconstruction, feelings so latently volatile that they could be triggered into the aggressive act of lynching, as if personal resentments could at once go unpunished and be relieved by collective action against one despised individual; the continuing political rivalry between Bourbon Democrats and the coalition of Republicans, Independents, and Greenbackers—an animosity fueled higher by the defeat of the Bourbons in the August elections; and the mad, sensual release of the moment (despite the widely reported solemnity and judicial deliberateness of the mob). Within these broad considerations lay subtle refinements and complex parts. Merely to isolate the evident components requires the realization that there were many inconsistencies and the understanding that, finally, the reasons were incongruously and violently interjoined, operating separately and together at the same time.

Inevitably, there were demands for an investigation.

Governor Rufus W. Cobb was at Helena in his home
county of Shelby helping take care of his sick wife.
Robert McKee—private secretary to Governor Cobb,
former editor of the Selma *Argus,* behind the scenes advisor to numerous public figures, and probably the most
respected man in Alabama politics, believed that even
though the chief executive was absent from Montgomery,
some official action was needed. On August 30 McKee,
acting in his capacity as private secretary, wrote a penetrating letter to George W. Taylor, solicitor of the first
judicial circuit. The letter became something of a *cause
célèbre* and required courage to write. Solicitor Taylor
received the communication and passed it on to various
Choctaw County officials who were not pleased with its
contents:

> DEAR SIR—The death of the negro Jack Turner at the
> hands of a mob in Choctaw county, the circumstances
> under which the lawless act was perpetrated, and the use
> that is being made of the affair, constitute an event of such
> gravity that the Governor deems it important to have,
> from the officers of the county charged therein with the
> enforcement of the law and the maintenance of the peace,
> a full report of all the facts in the case. No other recent
> event in the State has occasioned so much regret at home
> or has elsewhere excited so profound a feeling. The peace
> and dignity of the State are offended, the good name of
> the commonwealth suffers abroad, and the county is re-
> proached wherever the story is told. The law provides
> adequate punishment for every criminal act and estab-
> lishes all the necessary agencies for the administration of
> justice. Mob violence is lawlessness, to be deplored by
> every good citizen and to be resisted by every conservator
> of the peace. The act under consideration, notwithstanding
> the provocation unofficially reported, appears to be an
> aggravated one, for the victim was in the hands of the
> officers of justice, and in jail would have been as powerless

for the prosecution of the plans attributed to him as he is in the grave. He was murdered, and under circumstances that afford mendacious enemies of our people and section a pretext for attributing his death to political or race antipathies. The Governor understands, of course, that your official duties in such cases begin with the grand jury and end with the petit jury, and he knows you will fearlessly and faithfully discharge them; but he hopes, in the meantime, and promptly, you will take it upon yourself, asking the assistance of the county officers, to make a full investigation of the tragedy, and report the facts to him.[10]

Both before and after McKee's letter there were demands for an investigation. An impartial inquiry into the facts of the hanging was requested by defenders of the mob—they were convinced the hanging would be revealed as a necessary act—and by others equally certain that no conspiracy had existed. "We are not only willing to undergo an investigation, but demand one in order to be properly understood by the world," thundered the Butler *Courier*. "We do not ask to be believed on bare assertions, because we intend to prove the existence of the conspiracy beyond peradventure." There was a plot, "and the next term of our circuit court will convince the most prejudiced that we not only acted with prudence, but with extreme moderation." [11] A Black Belt journal, the Greensboro *Alabama Beacon,* while sympathizing strongly with the white people of Choctaw County, still demanded an investigation. "The whites owe it to themselves," its editor wrote, "and to the people of the South generally, to have the affair fully and thoroughly investigated, and the facts, which go to prove the conspiracy,

10.   Robert W. McKee to George W. Taylor, August 30, 1882, Governor Rufus W. Cobb's Letter Book, June, 1882–November, 1882, pp. 270, 272. The letter was widely circulated in Alabama newspapers.
11.   Butler *Courier,* August 30, 1882.

and to justify the course they pursued, published to the world." The *Alabama Beacon,* which was the only newspaper to draw a parallel between Jack Turner's activities and those of the Virginia slave Nat Turner fifty-one years earlier, continued: "That they had good grounds for doing what they did, we most confidently believe. Nor do we believe there is a community in the North, that would not have taken the law in their hands under like circumstances." [12]

One of the state's most powerful Bourbon newspapers, the Mobile *Daily Register,* remarked, "There can be no objection to . . . an investigation. What the people of Alabama desire is truth and justice." [13] Answering critics who feared for the safety of the other prisoners, an editor in Choctaw County declared, "We want them to live, and to have a trial; because we believe their conviction in a court is the only possible way in which the full force of our evidence as to the reality of the conspiracy can be brought to bear on the minds of the public. We have done nothing wrong; but we have been shamefully belied, and most unaccountably and unreasonably suspected." [14]

If the defenders of the hanging seemed to welcome an inquiry, those who denounced the deed insisted on one. In an editorial captioned "Turn on the Light," the Huntsville *Gazette* declared, "The colored people of this State and of the country at large are not satisfied that such a great crime as that charged upon their people and race in Choctaw County should go uninvestigated." The journal wanted every detail examined. "This people are charged with forming a conspiracy to murder indiscriminately

12. Greensboro *Alabama Beacon,* September 8, 1882.
13. Mobile *Daily Register,* September 1, 1882.
14. Butler *Courier,* September 13, 1882.

their white fellow citizens, men, women and children. On this charge the leading colored citizen of the county has without any show of a defense, without judge or jury, been publicly lynched and published to the world." Simple justice to the black race warranted an official inquiry. "Let the State order the investigation. If it [is] fair and impartial and establishes the guilt of Jack Turner and his people the colored people will yield to none in the strongest condemnation. If they have been grossly and wrongfully slandered as reason and every circumstance indicates then they are entitled to a lawful redress and the fullest exoneration." [15]

Various Northern newspapers did not believe the affair would be examined in detail. The New York *Times* held out no hope for action by state courts, and since the federal courts had no jurisdiction unless a national election was involved, the paper hoped the results of the upcoming congressional race would be contested before the House of Representatives.[16] Calling for a thorough airing of the entire episode, the Chicago *Inter Ocean* was, nevertheless, dubious about the results: "As society is organized in that part of the country, it is doubtful whether it is possible to secure proper punishment for crimes committed by white people against black." [17]

Despite their concern, people outside of Alabama were less involved with the Choctaw County affair than were native citizens. A number of Alabamians refused to accept with resignation what had occurred. Signing himself "One of the Crew," a black man wrote a plaintive letter couched in moving religious phrases and asking, in effect,

15. Huntsville *Gazette*, September 9, 1882.
16. New York *Times*, August 28, 1882.
17. Chicago *Inter Ocean*, September 2, 1882.

for mercy from the Lord and the state of Alabama. He explained that the colored people had worked hard, and if anyone wondered what his people wanted, *"We* ask but an equal chance before the law, no more, *no less.* . . . Now, we ask you, for the fair name of your State, for the good of humanity, and for the cause of Him that you profess to serve, to frown down on such murderers as those of Jack Turner. . . . Will you not, at least, frown down those whose hands are red with the blood of our murdered?" [18]

Matching the eloquence of "One of the Crew" were the searching editorials of L. W. Grant, the fiercely independent editor of the hill country Jacksonville *Republican* in Calhoun County. Although not without its own gentry, Jacksonville was mainly populated by moderately prosperous whites. Speculating about the results of an investigation, Grant raised a chilling question for his fellow whites: "Suppose the paper on which they hung that man should turn out to be the forgery of some foolish wag, or worse, of some evil disposed person who wished to bring the men in it into trouble? How then will the good men of Choctaw feel who took part with the mob in the execution of the negro man? What now seems a righteous judgment would turn out to be murder." [19]

In Greene, a neighboring Black Belt county that had seen more than its share of racial violence, a Democratic editor was chagrined at what an investigation into the hanging of Jack Turner would reveal. "It would show that a man had been hung without being allowed a trial by a jury of his countrymen, or to introduce a witness to

18. See letter in Huntsville *Gazette,* September 22, 1882.
19. Jacksonville *Republican,* September 2, 1882.

testify in his behalf, or to be heard by himself or counsel
—without the color even of judicial proceedings." [20]

Meeting at night in the United States courtroom at
Montgomery, a number of blacks issued a formal demand
for an investigation. With James K. Greene presiding, the
members drafted and forwarded a petition to Governor
Cobb. They pointed out that "Extraordinary public evils
justify extraordinary public action" and asked the chief
executive to appoint a four-member commission (composed of members of both parties) to go to Choctaw
County and determine the facts of the hanging. "As citizens," the petitioners continued, "we deprecate the existence of all race hatred and prejudices between the whites
and blacks, as fatal to the prosperity of both classes, and,
therefore, if the aforesaid charge is untrue, as we believe
it to be, we wish our people vindicated before the world,
or if it is true, we wish to assert our solemn disclaimer
that any such animus was known by us to exist in the
heart of a single member of our race. In the interest of a
common people and for the good of a common country,
we wish the above investigation to be made." [21]

The strongest condemnation of the hanging came from
the Arthur Republican Club, comprised mainly of Negroes living in Mobile. Meeting August 25, with President Charles Hurley presiding, the members acted on
"information having reached us of the unlawful arrests,

20. Camden *News and Pacificator,* October 6, 1882, quoting
Eutaw *Mirror.*

21. Proceedings quoted in Mobile *Daily Register,* September 1,
1882. See also Montgomery *Advertiser,* August 30–31, 1882; Marion
Commonwealth, September 7, 1882. The bipartisan committee was to
consist of Chief Justice Robert Brickell of the supreme court of Alabama; Peter Hamilton of Mobile; George Turner of Montgomery; and
D. D. Shelby of Madison County.

inhuman beating of a large number of our colored Republican brethren, and of the diabolical and cold blooded murder of Jack Turner, a leading colored Republican at Butler . . . by the so-called citizens of Choctaw county, Alabama." Because of such events, "We . . . do hereby denounce such outrageous, blood-thirsty and inhuman proceedings." Moreover, "We hereby denounce the so-called insurrection as fabulous and devoid of any truth. We further denounce the murderers of the late Jack Turner as falsifiers of the truth, and their inhuman and brutal conduct without a parallel in the history of our country. We further denounce them as foul, cold-blooded, premeditated murderers." The Arthur Club's resolutions were forwarded to President Chester A. Arthur, the secretaries of state and of war, and the attorney general with the request that the United States government investigate and prosecute "the murderers and law-breakers of Choctaw County." Such resolutions, a Democratic writer warned, should not be taken too seriously. Arthur Club members, after all, were "imbued with race prejudices and political passions engendered and kept alive by leaders reckless of all that is good and steeped to the scalp locks in all that is villainous and low." [22]

While the demands for an investigation were being made, the issue of politics intruded and became the single most important factor in the aftermath of the hanging—with results that were bitterly ironic. Considering Jack Turner's active role in Republican politics in Choctaw County and the First Congressional District, it was inevitable that his party would view the hanging as an act of political intimidation. That the Democrats might use

22. Montgomery *Advertiser,* August 30, 31, 1882.

the tragedy for their own political advantage might seem far-fetched, but such was the case. Anticipating a political attack, Bourbon defenders quickly executed the simple but effective maneuver of discrediting the opposition. With classic skill they employed a broad, one-sided use of history. Who, they asked, were the critics of the hanging? None other than the hated carpetbaggers and scalawags of recent Reconstruction fame. How could the participants and directors of such a thoroughly corrupt debacle be believed? In fact, the Radicals themselves were probably responsible for the hanging and planned to exploit it for political profit. By turning the attack back on the attackers, the defenders hoped to divert public criticism from themselves. Besides dismissing their detractors with the cry of "consider the source," Democrats accused the Republicans of creating a situation that made the act of violence inevitable. Denying that politics was in any way connected with Jack Turner's hanging, the Bourbons charged that the Republicans, nonetheless, were callously using it for political purposes. The strategy was brilliant—the Bourbons succeeded in wrapping their own politics in a blanket of self-righteous denial that was safe from attack.

The Democratic congressional convention, which proved to be an extended one, met at Jackson in Clarke County on August 21. It is not certain that all of the delegates had heard of the hanging when they assembled, but before adjournment was gaveled, the event and its influence on the election were central to most conversations. Chairman J. Little Smith of Mobile maintained order as the struggle unfolded among incumbent Thomas H. Herndon of Mobile, Charles L. Scott of Monroe County, and S. T. Prince of Choctaw County. In a sense the competition was that of the rural counties versus Mobile, and under the two-thirds majority rule, voting went on for 243 ballots. After two days the weary delegates finally agreed that the low man would be dropped after the fifth ballot. Prince's name was withdrawn after the fourth ballot, and on the sixth Herndon was renominated—249 ballots after the voting had begun.[23] When the politicians returned to their homes, they did so with the determination to win, but there was little reason for confidence.

The Republican nominating convention was not held until September 5. The gathering of blacks and a few whites at Mobile was presided over by Frank H. Threat, the Negro of Demopolis who had remained faithful to the party despite previous disappointments. There was little dispute over the nominee as the convention moved quickly to name Luther R. Smith. The man chosen to oppose Herndon was well known as a carpetbagger who had moved to Choctaw County shortly after the end of the Civil War. Combining farming with politics, Smith, who would be branded "Lucifer Radical Smith" by the Bourbons, was appointed to the Board of Registration and moved from there to election to the state legislature. He resigned from the legislature and served two terms as the able judge of the circuit court. Although a political friend and ally of Jack Turner, Judge Smith had handed down decisions against the Negro, and could hardly be accused of having sacrificed justice in order to court favor with his black followers. Yet the dead leader had respected Smith and would have campaigned vigorously for him. In

23. Mobile *Daily Register,* August 24, 1882; Butler *Courier,* August 30, 1882; Grove Hill *Clarke County Democrat,* August 30, 1882.

any case, the Republicans had easily nominated their best man.[24]

Jack Turner's death greatly influenced the deliberations of the Republican convention. W. D. Wickersham, a white man and former postmaster of Mobile, wanted the tragedy to be "made the *key note* of the campaign." J. W. Burke, collector of the Port of Mobile and chairman of the Republican district executive committee, agreed. Philip Joseph, black editor of the Mobile *Gazette,* introduced a resolution expressing the collective feeling of the delegates and one that was overwhelmingly adopted: "That the base, atrocious and cowardly murder of Jack Turner and the torture of other leading colored Republicans of Choctaw County on account of their devotion to the Republican opposition to the Democratic party are crimes the heinousness of which finds no parallel in the rolls of human infamy." [25]

In the opinion of the Democrats, the main results of the Radical convention were that "the white people were denounced, and the race issue thrust upon our people." [26] As for Philip Joseph, his "set of clap-trap resolutions" was no more than a "strong effort to make political capital of the lynching of Jack Turner." [27]

The confused situation in Choctaw County had come down to the numerous demands for an investigation—de-

24. For details of the convention see Mobile *Daily Register,* September 6–8, 1882. An extremely critical biographical sketch of Judge Smith may be found in Butler *Courier,* October 7, 1882.

25. A special election pamphlet was circulated by Democrats in Mobile just prior to the election. The four-page document praised Herndon while scoring the Republicans as unworthy of respect. The publication is microfilmed with the Mobile *Daily Register* for the year 1882, hereinafter cited as Special Election Pamphlet.

26. Special Election Pamphlet.

27. Demopolis *Marengo News-Journal,* September 9, 1882.

mands that were made simultaneously with an acrimonious political canvass that influenced the direction and
results of the inquiry. There also remained the important
business of trying the accused—or so it would seem. As
it turned out, the only real investigation, outside the one
conducted by the grand jury, that indicted the alleged
conspirators, was a reply to Private Secretary McKee's
letter issued by county officials on September 4 and forwarded to Montgomery. The official reply plus the arguments offered by individuals and Bourbon newspapers
formed the basic case for the defense. In opposition were
individuals and journals who spoke for Jack Turner. The
results were significant.

6

Seekers of the Truth

THE DEFENDERS OF Jack Turner's hanging poured forth a stream of arguments justifying his murder as well as the means. Basic to their case was the thesis that the plot had existed. It followed, therefore, that group action had been essential to forestall the massacre of the white people—*all* of them, or, as numerous writers put it, the Caucasians of Choctaw County would have been slaughtered from the cradle to the grave.

Most defenders went beyond the New Orleans *Times-Democrat* which reasoned that since the hanging had occurred and been carried out by white men, then it was certain that there had to be *some* justification. Without pretending to know any of the facts, the *Times-Democrat* declared, "We can safely conclude . . . that the whole population of Choctaw county would not have acted as they did unless there was some grave reason for it." [1]

With several variations, the justifications focused on a number of basic themes. One argument concerned the general nature of the black man—a sweeping, highly partisan examination of his character, psychological makeup,

1. New Orleans *Times-Democrat,* August 22, 1882.

and his place in history and society. A second case, one repeatedly made, was that the people had no choice once their very lives were threatened, and that they acted to preserve hearth and home. Used in conjunction with this hypothesis was the explanation that the people were overcome by emotions and acted hastily, in the heat of the moment. Amplified and embellished, this argument evoked grisly and horrifying flights of prose among the defenders that not only made the mob's action excusable but praiseworthy, and beyond that lay the groundwork for any future action. Emerging as a third part of the defenders' hanging manual was the flat assertion that the documents disclosing the details of the plot were authentic (there were several closely related incidents and circumstances that helped expand this argument). Important to all of the justifications, and forming a separate category unto itself, was the issue of politics. Finally, there was the fifth and ultimate justification: Jack Turner. If it could be established that Jack had about him the essence of evil, that he was a cruel savage not only incapable of rational behavior, but a fiend obsessed with gaining bloody revenge on the white race, then the mob had acted wisely and nobly. To this end all manner of supposedly unimpeachable evidence garnered from all manner of sources, equally unimpeachable, was brought forward and paraded before the public. As the acknowledged leader of his people, Jack Turner was capable of translating his murderous fury into action—something that could not be permitted, whatever the cost.

In explaining the specific tragedy at Butler, there were those who employed the first area of defense. They addressed themselves to the larger issue of the "typical"

Negro, the Black Everyman. An explanation of what He was like would go far toward producing an understanding of why the hanging at Butler in the August sun had been necessary. A Florida citizen, residing in Pensacola, was not speaking only for himself when he wrote that deep in the heart of every black lay an antipathy toward every white. These malevolent feelings made the black man forever dangerous. In the writer's words, "The negro, true to his barbaric instincts like the Indian, will not tolerate the presence of the white race and saxon civilization, except under such conditions as render it impossible for him to carry out his ever present purpose to destroy the race and civilization that in the bottom of his heart he hates. Thinking men in the North, *all* honest men in the South, recognize the truth of this, and only the mad and reckless ambition and desire for political power prevents its universal recognition." [2]

If the Black Everyman harbored such latent hostility, then it was not difficult to believe that a person with the guile and craft of Jack Turner could rally his people to revolution. In fact, one did not have to accept the theory completely in order to see that the evil genius of Jack Turner could manifest itself. "The great majority of the negroes [in] Alabama are well disposed," one white man wrote. "But there is another class of negroes, who instigated by the devil and with malicious cunningness, are and have been at all times willing and ready to concoct any scheme, and do anything to '*put down the whites*' (as they call it)." [3]

According to the Butler *Courier,* "The slave is the

2. Pensacola *Semi-Weekly Commercial,* August 25, 1882.
3. Opelika *Times,* August 25, 1882.

same in all countries and is actuated by the same feelings of revenge against his former owners." [4] The question might logically have been raised if such a generalization could be applied to Jack Turner. For one thing, his former master, B. L. Turner, was dead, and for another, the strongest bonds of friendship, not feelings of revenge, had joined the two men. But such a question was not posed, and it was argued by many that a deep hatred of whites was embedded in Jack Turner's psyche. "This is the theory on which the conspiracy was conceived," the *Courier* speculated, "and this would have nerved him with the boldness to attempt its execution." [5] Having laid down the broad premise that black men wanted to destroy white men (although the hypothesis was shaky and indefensible, it was not seriously doubted), the defenders moved on to their other arguments.

The point would be made repeatedly that since the so-called plotters were under lock and key, the normal channels of justice were open and rendered hanging unnecessary. Since this was so, the necessity of protecting homes and families by violence could not be defended. Not true, the defenders of the lynching replied. The *Examiner,* published in Hayneville, county seat of the Black Belt polity of Lowndes, offered vigorous and bizarre rebuttal. Admitting that there were better ways to adjudicate crime than by mob law, and that whipping a prisoner to gain a confession was wrong, the journal still thought it proper for the people to substitute their will

4. Butler *Courier,* September 6, 1882.
5. *Ibid.* The *Courier* hinted broadly that Jack's malignant feelings against whites were especially pronounced because "he is a scion of the same stock." If the paper meant that Jack was partly white, it was in error. The point may have been that he shared the same surname as B. L. Turner.

for the state law governing the crime of conspiracy. The people had substituted hanging. "And they are not to be really censured for it. If they were fully satisfied with the evidence of his guilt they were right to hang the murderous scoundrel as a warning to his fellow plotters." For that matter, the *Examiner* had little confidence in the state's juries. "They are far more likely to acquit the right man than a mob is to hang the wrong man." [6]

After Robert McKee wrote his critical letter in behalf of Governor Cobb, the Hayneville *Examiner* defined its position more clearly. "What gabble is it to talk of the forms of the law when the torch and the knife of the midnight assassin is at your door?" the paper asked. "The people of Choctaw did precisely what the people of Mobile, or Paris, or Berlin would have done. And they have the fullest sympathy and endorsement of every man who does not crouch and tremble at the fear of Yankee censure. God bless the people of Choctaw!" [7]

The Mobile *Daily Register* was disturbed by the trouble in Choctaw County, and while "it culminated in a retribution which all law-abiding citizens must deplore and condemn, but which no one, with the facts as they have been published before him, can say was not deserved by the conspirators against our peace and lives." It seemed a shame to the port city's newspaper that government witnesses might be called to testify against "citizens who are all guilty of no further crime than that of defending their homes and families from rapine and slaughter." [8]

"A more diabolical plot was never concocted" was the studied judgment of the Montgomery *Advertiser*. Al-

6. Hayneville *Examiner*, September 6, 1882.
7. *Ibid.*, September 20, 1882.
8. Mobile *Daily Register*, September 17, 20, 1882.

though not approving of lynching, the paper accepted the fact of Jack Turner's death, and wanted the co-conspirators to be sentenced to jail. "It is a case where temporising with crime will be a crime in itself." A few days later the *Advertiser* admitted that the hanging was not only carried out too quickly and without sufficient evidence, but was unnecessary. Torturing the prisoners was wrong, and the state's image had been damaged. "But we can also appreciate the influences that swayed the . . . citizens of Choctaw County, and they shall not be villified without a protest from us." [9]

The Demopolis *Marengo News-Journal* found it difficult to justify mob law even in the most extreme and extraordinary emergencies. "And yet there are cases in which the popular judgment seems to be that society must protect itself by summary action." Every law-abiding citizen should deplore conditions which rendered necessary or possible the tragedy at Butler. "But what could the good people of Choctaw do? Must they rest with folded hands and suffer themselves, their wives and little ones to be butchered by a fiend incarnate and his followers. Self protection is said to be the first law of nature and it is plain that this law was invoked by these people under the firm conviction that the most imminent danger existed and a pressing necessity for immediate action." [10]

Considering the varied people involved in the hanging, and taking cognizance of their desire to preserve their homes, the Selma *Times* reasoned that the action at Butler had been illegal only in the most technical sense. "When we consider the number of citizens, their charac-

9. Montgomery *Advertiser*, August 23, 31, 1882.
10. Demopolis *Marengo News-Journal*, August 26, 1882.

ter, the mixture of races, the time and method selected, it was not in spirit and process . . . a triumph of mob law. It was the majesty of justice, and can have no evil effect." [11]

A modification of the protection-of-the-homes thesis was that the people had acted on impulse, that they had been overcome by the passions of the moment. Contending that it was "not the advocate of mob law under any circumstances, deplores any resort to it and would, if possible, remove forever from this country all cause for or possibility of its occurrence," the Birmingham *Iron Age* found itself in a painful position. How and why had such a large group of citizens participated in mob action? The paper conceded that "the act may have been imprudent, unwise, ill-advised, criminal, and too hasty," but refused to denounce the participants in the summary proceedings "as red-handed assassins and cold blooded murderers." Instead, the incident was an anomaly, an isolated affair not likely to be repeated, an "uprising of a law-respecting and abiding, but outraged and indignant people who, for the once, take the law into their own hands and administer justice." [12]

As the Bourbons became increasingly critical of Governor Cobb's position relative to the hanging, contending that the duly chosen Democratic governor of the state was, by his actions, actually aiding the Republican cause in the upcoming election, the chief executive's role proved embarrassing. A letter signed "High Private," appeared in the Montgomery *Advertiser* on August 31. The letter, openly acknowledged as having been written by Robert McKee, attempted to modify some of the state-

11. Quoted in Butler *Courier*, August 30, 1882.
12. Birmingham *Iron Age*, September 21, 1882.

ments contained in the earlier official letter to Solicitor Taylor. The private secretary, although trying to relieve some of the pressure on Governor Cobb, attempted to salvage what he could by continuing to champion universal principles of justice. At the same time "High Private" sought to deprecate all efforts by Republicans to reap political gain from the affair, and in any case, the letter was decidedly not the high point in McKee's otherwise distinguished career. McKee contended that the facts of the case did not "tend to show that [Jack Turner] was hung because he was a negro or because he was a Republican." Intending to exonerate, at least partially, the Choctaw countians, McKee explained that "In a moment of madness, or of panic, the people of Choctaw have committed an act which is deplored by every good citizen, and which rejoices only the Republican leaders, who are using the tragedy for all that can be made out of it, by the most shameless misrepresentations, and the most deliberate exaggeration." [13]

A Talladega journalist considered the tortures indefensible and the hanging unwarranted, but still could not brand the participants as murderers. It was simply that "in considering matters of this kind due allowance must be made for the surroundings." He observed, "The people of Choctaw county were suddenly led to believe that themselves, their wives and little ones had been doomed to butchery by a wide spread conspiracy that found a red-handed conspirator standing close to every hearth-stone ready to strike. The diabolism of the scheme was calculated to arouse the wildest passion at its merest mention, and at once banish reason and judgment." The hanging occurred because a frightened people momentarily lost

13. Montgomery *Advertiser*, August 31, 1882.

control. "Men were in no condition to weigh the evidence, and under the strong impulse of the moment were carried beyond the limits prescribed by law." [14]

In Choctaw County the white people who condoned the hanging acknowledged the support they were receiving and denounced their detractors. In general they agreed with the protection-of-the-homes concept but denied that they had been overcome by passion. The Butler *Courier,* for example, approved of the mob's action whereby the people "did not hesitate under the theory of self-protection to become a law unto themselves. Technically speaking, it may have been unlawful, but under the spirit and intention of all laws it was eminently proper and right." The suggestion that the people momentarily lost control and hanged Jack Turner out of "excitement and fear" was dismissed as "meaningless slander." "Conscious of right," one Choctaw countian wrote, "we fear neither lies, slanders, misconceptions nor courts. We acted in good faith with calmness and deliberation and can set ourselves right before the forum of the world." Stated more briefly, "No people could have behaved better, and no people ever showed more magnanimity under excessive aggravation than the people of Choctaw County throughout this entire trouble." [15]

Not even the Butler *Courier* defended the hanging episode with the vehemence of the Carrollton *West Alabamian.* For sheer hyperbolic intensity the *West Alabamian,* published in the Black Belt county of Pickens, was unrivaled. Its editor denied that a crowd numbering in the hundreds would calmly and deliberately hang a man without cause. That a mob spurred into hasty and irre-

14. Talladega *Our Mountain Home,* September 6, 1882.
15. Butler *Courier,* August 30, September 6, 1882.

sponsible action by the excitement of rape or murder
would do so was neither improbable nor infrequent. But
the event at Butler was different. Instead of a mob com-
mitting a sudden, lawless, and unpremediated deed, "it
was the gathering together, on a set day of the 'bone and
sinew,' the manhood, the citizenship of nearly a *whole*
law-abiding county, to consider the gravest question
which can ever arise before men, viz: the preservation of
themselves, their wives and little ones, from a common
and indiscriminate massacre, in cold blood, by pitiless,
hellish brutes in human shape. This and nothing more—
to them a vital all-absorbing question. What they did to
avert the threatened calamity was performed cooly, dis-
passionately and conscientiously, after a careful investigation of facts and evidence, while their frightened wives
and children awaited, tremblingly, their return home." [16]

Despite the almost hysterical rhetoric of the defenders,
their arguments about protecting themselves from a terrible fate did not hold up. That many of the people *believed* they were defending their homes was, however,
true. A Northern paper admitted as much by writing a
story under the headline EDGEFIELD ECLIPSED. The reference was to Edgefield County, South Carolina, which
had "hitherto enjoyed the reputation of being the scarriest
county in the whole south on the subject of the security
of whites against blacks. Henceforth Choctaw County,
Alabama, is entitled to the palm." [17] A caustic New
England editor remarked that Negro revolutions were
nonexistent, and, "In the slaughtering business the white
men of the South have had an uninterrupted monop-

16. Carrollton *West Alabamian*, September 20, 1882.
17. Linden *Reporter*, September 1, 1882, quoting New York
Herald. For conditions in Edgefield see George Brown Tindall,
South Carolina Negroes 1877–1900 (Columbia, 1952), 26–28, 32.

oly." [18] In a bitingly sarcastic editorial the New York *Times* agreed that Jack Turner and the blacks had engineered a conspiracy, only "277 years 6 weeks and 6 days after the discovery of the gunpowder plot, upon which their own horrid plan was plainly modeled." The entire affair was most fortunate and humane. In fact, Jack Turner "was comfortably, decently, and in the most orderly manner, hanged. Choctaw County was delivered from its blood-curdling perils, babes slept that night in sweet serenity, the women returned to their knitting and the men to their liquor." [19]

By any yardstick Choctaw was not a typical Black Belt county. The blacks outnumbered the whites by scarcely more than a thousand, and it was the whites who held the position of power. Jack Turner had proved that organization and leadership could produce a political revolt, but the county was hardly the place for blacks to stage a successful physical revolt through sheer force. "The 7,387 white inhabitants of Choctaw county make too large a demand upon the credulity of the people of the United States in this story," the New York *Herald* asserted.[20] The declaration that the people had acted in self-defense also drew fire from Washington. Knowledgeable of conditions in Choctaw County, an observer in the capitol considered the existence of a plot "sufficiently absurd to create disbelief in the minds of any who are familiar with the habits and characteristics of the two races in that locality." [21]

Shortly after the hanging, George Turner, the white

18. Hartford *Courant,* August 22, 1882.
19. New York *Times,* August 23, 1882.
20. Quoted in Linden *Reporter,* September 1, 1882.
21. Chicago *Inter Ocean,* August 25, 1882, quoting a lengthy telegram from Washington, D.C., dated August 23.

leader in Alabama's Republican party, who was despised by the Democrats as a carpetbagger, appeared in New York. Formerly a United States marshal at Mobile and then chairman of the Republican state executive committee, he was well acquainted with Jack Turner—especially since the hearings in Mobile concerning Manning and Carnathan. The visitor from the South was interviewed by the New York *Times* concerning Jack Turner and affairs in Choctaw County. Pointing out that he knew the black people well, George Turner contended that the plot had been invented. Such a conspiracy was impossible by a people who had "endured wrongs and cruelties for centuries in this country," and more than that, a people who had "endured these things with an unequaled patience." To believe that a plot existed was to strain common sense and was "laughed at as absurd by the colored people themselves." [22] But could the Republican politician be believed? Emphatically not, the Democrats replied. One Bourbon writer declared that George Turner's status as "a carpetbagger is sufficient to discredit him, as all carpetbaggers are necessarily liars." [23]

Disposing of native Alabamians who were critical of the hanging was not so easy. A Pike County newspaper that printed the original Associated Press story soon declared that even the fear of a Negro insurrection in Choctaw County or anywhere else in Alabama was groundless.[24] From his newspaper office in Jacksonville,

22. New York *Times*, August 26, 1882.
23. Hayneville *Examiner*, September 6, 1882. For similar viewpoints see Mobile *Daily Register*, September 9, 1882; Tuskaloosa *Gazette*, September 7, 1882. The Montgomery *Advertiser*, September 1, 1882, dismissed Turner by declaring, "The whole interview is a foul distorting of facts to the purposes of a party."
24. Troy *Enquirer*, September 16, 1882.

L. W. Grant continued to write powerful editorials in the weekly *Republican*. With cold logic, Grant wondered why the evidence and those arrested had not been turned over to the courts for investigation. "The death of the negro Turner was not necessary to the suppression of the threatened outbreak," Grant wrote. "The arrest of supposed ringleaders would have affected this. The people of Choctaw county have made a mistake. They have taken life on the most flimsy testimony. There is the terrible possibility that an innocent man has been hung. Mob law is the wrong remedy." [25]

The Huntsville *Gazette,* whose motto was "With Charity for All, and Malice Towards None," was angered by statements that at last conditions were quiet in Choctaw County. The *Gazette*'s Negro editor agreed that this was so, but at what cost? "Peace reigns in Choctaw—the peace of Warsaw." [26] One white Alabamian of Lee County (who signed himself "Brett") wrote a letter to the Opelika *Times*. "Why don't you come out against this Judge Lynch business?" he wondered. "Come out and denounce it as it should be denounced. It is a slur upon the civilization of the country. A disgrace upon Alabama and her citizenship that mob rule has such sway." [27] Equally penetrating sentiments were contained in a private letter that found its way into the Montgomery *Advertiser*. The author, who had carefully reviewed all of the material available on the hanging, was ashamed, puzzled, disappointed, and bitter: "Can such things happen in our midst? The crime was great, with which they

25. Jacksonville *Republican,* September 2, 1882.
26. Huntsville *Gazette,* September 9, 1882. The same issue entitled an editorial "Choctaw Outrage Against Humanity." See also *ibid.,* September 2, 1882.
27. Opelika *Times,* September 8, 1882.

were charged. But our race has battled for a thousand years against the practice of 'torturing' prisoners to make them 'squeal.' " He added, "The press should unsparingly denounce and rebuke this lawless, cruel, demon spirit of mob law which is growing up in our midst. . . . It is no excuse to say they conspired to perpetrate a great crime. There is but one way to find out[:] in a court of law." [28]

The third defense, one believed by many, was that the incriminating documents constituted irrefutable evidence that the conspiracy had existed. The grand jury heard a number of witnesses who claimed familiarity with the handwriting of the accused men. George E. Nettles, an employee at a store where Fred Barney traded, believed that at least two of the documents had been signed by the Negro teacher. "I cannot swear positively that he wrote these papers but my best judgment & belief is that they are his signatures." H. L. Gaines, unable to correlate any signatures and unable to say if he had ever sold Fred Barney any paper of the type upon which the documents were written, focused attention on the use of the word *mens* in the papers. He had, Gaines averred, frequently called Fred Barney's attention to the misuse of the word, adding that the black still insisted on using *mens* instead of *men*. The statement did not seem sufficient evidence to warrant returning a true bill, and Gaines admitted that such usage was "a very common error with negroes." [29]

All of the witnesses testified that the documents had been written by at least three different persons. One man declared that he recognized Jack Turner's handwriting, and T. A. Hightower, an alleged participant in the tor-

28. Montgomery *Advertiser*, August 30, 1882.
29. Choctaw County Grand Jury Proceedings, Fall, 1882, and Spring, 1883, Circuit Clerk's Office. Physical deterioration of the Proceedings has made some of the witnesses' names unreadable.

turing of Willis Lyman, claiming he had seen Jack write his name numerous times, was "confident" that the documents contained his signature. J. J. Kelly told the grand jury, "I am acquainted with the handwriting of Jesse Wilson—have seen it frequently. I think the papers shown are in Jesse Wilson's handwriting." In agreement was another witness: "I am acquainted with Jesse Wilson's hand-writing—and I am as positive about his almost as if I had seen him write it." [30]

In its report to Governor Cobb the special committee in Choctaw County carefully avoided mentioning that two of the prisoners had been tortured. For the most part, the report condensed and summarized the testimony presented to the grand jury. In appending evidence related to the documents, the special committee made several points: one of the leaders (Jim Roberts, who was taken into custody some time after the initial arrests) was seen riding repeatedly over the road near the spot where the papers were found on the day of their discovery; there were signs of a secret meeting at the campground; several of the suspected parties had fled; a large amount of gunpowder had been discovered on the premises of one of the suspects; the papers themselves had been found near the campground, the very place where the massacre was to begin; the papers had been discovered and disclosed by Greenbackers instead of Democrats; Willis Lyman, the paid agent of the conspirators, lived at Butler, yet he was in the neighborhood of Desotoville when the papers were found and was arrested there; several Negroes had been visited by other blacks and induced to contradict "their first statements voluntarily made." [31]

30. *Ibid.*, 103, 105, 107.
31. Special Citizens' Report.

These arguments seemed less impressive when exposed to closer examination. Jim Roberts' presence on the road near Allen's Mill proved nothing. People were always trooping in and out of the campground, and there was no evidence that any of the accused men had been there. Considering the fate of Jack Turner, the flight of several of those suspected could easily be interpreted as acts of self-preservation. The suspect who owned the gunpowder made the reasonable explanation that he intended to use it for hunting purposes. That the documents were found in the proximity of where the plot was to begin lost some of its ominous flavor when it was recalled that they were discovered while the contemplated act was over a month away. The calico-tied papers were placed so conspicuously in the road that sooner or later they would have been found. Their disposition by Brown, the McCalls, and others was normal and might have been expected of any good citizens. What was important was who placed the papers there, not who discovered them.

Willis Lyman had every right to be in the Desotoville neighborhood if he so chose, and his being there hardly constituted a conspiracy. Declarations that witnesses who contradicted earlier statements proved the existence of a plot amounted to spurious reasoning. The defense was simply frustrated when statements made by some of the witnesses (some thirty-five were called by the grand jury, although not all testified) failed to coincide with what they were expected to say. When several who took the stand declared emphatically that they knew nothing of the plot, they were quickly excused. Others spoke at greater length, but the sum of their remarks was that though they knew Jack Turner and the others, they had never heard of any proposed massacre of the whites.

Other than the documents themselves, the defenders had no tangible proof of a plot. Increasingly they employed the broad argument that the letters had to have been written by Negroes. As one editor explained, "The papers themselves are as distinctively and unmistakably negro as the kinky head and black skin, and no one having the slightest knowledge of negro character could doubt, after reading the papers, that they were conceived and executed by the brain of a negro." [32] Several of those appearing before the grand jury, although unable to make positive comparisons of the handwriting, took pains to say that from their insight into the Negro's nature, his speech patterns, and his penmanship, the papers had been written by black men. As one witness typically said, "I am satisfied beyond a doubt from my general knowledge of the negro character & from the writing, language, composition, & orthography of these papers that they were composed & written by negroes." [33]

The documents, although vigorously defended as final proof of the conspiracy, were open to serious challenge. George Turner, Alabama's white Republican leader, pointed out that the black people were not expert writers and the papers could have easily been forged.[34] Certainly native white Southerners who wished to do so could have written some convincing documents. The papers contained several references to the "Invasion of Butler" in 1874, and always in the context of a plot that had been thwarted but one that would be successful on September 17. Since there had been no plot in 1874, the reference to one was obviously not made by Jack Turner and the

32. Butler *Courier,* August 30, 1882.
33. Choctaw County Grand Jury Proceedings, Fall, 1882, and Spring, 1883, p. 108.
34. Quoted in New York *Times,* August 26, 1882.

Negroes but by forgers. The attempt was to establish the existence of an on-going plot. There was also the question of why the documents covered such a brief span of time. For a scheme of long duration to be documented for only a matter of weeks seemed strange, and the defense's case that there were other unfound papers was weak. Since the organization was supposedly founded in 1878, it would have been difficult to forge four years of minutes.

Some of the witnesses before the grand jury had their doubts about the documents. Even those willing to make positive statements did so with certain reservations and equivocations. One man familiar with Jack Turner's signature said that the "c" in Jack and the "T" in Turner as revealed by the papers were different from Jack's usual handwriting. "I do not think they are the same hand-writing." C. C. McCall, who had carried the papers to Solicitor Taylor at Mount Sterling, said "My impression at first was that the papers were genuine. This impression remained with me only a short time. I changed my opinion between Tuesday & Saturday when Jack was hung." [35]

The very existence of the papers strained credulity. Why would the blacks jeopardize the realization of their goal by maintaining incriminating evidence? The New York *Times* and the Atlanta *Constitution* were dubious about rural Negroes keeping minutes. "It seems incredible that negroes should plot to murder the whites," the *Constitution* declared. Beyond that "it is more incredible still that they should make a record of their purposes." According to the *Times*, "Alabama negroes plotting the massacre of a county full of white folks would have about

35. Choctaw County Grand Jury Proceedings, Fall, 1882, and Spring, 1883, p. 109.

as much use for 'papers' as a pig would have for a fine-toothed comb." Dismissing the "circumstantial story" as one of "palpable falsity," the *Times* did not believe any man in his senses could accept the story that the blacks had concocted a paper plot to murder whites.[36]

It appears certain that the papers were expertly forged and placed where they were certain to be found. Without excusing the lynching of Jack Turner, it is possible to see how many people were manipulated into violating the most basic principles of justice. They were tricked into thinking that the documents were genuine and that the conspiracy existed.

In a special way the fourth defense, that of politics, found its way into the rationalization for the hanging of Jack Turner. But politics became as well a weapon for the people and parties who, personally and abstractly, wanted to see the Negro leader vindicated. The political turmoil that followed the hanging is discussed in the following chapter.

Perhaps the most blatantly emotional defense centered around the discussions of Jack Turner as a man, as an individual who in slightly more than four decades (over half of his life was spent as a slave) had achieved such notoriety as to force his fellow citizens to end his life on a makeshift gallows. For their clinching argument the special committee advised Governor Cobb to consider "the character of Jack Turner." His court record before the circuit and county courts dating back to 1872 and going through 1881 was listed. Continuing, the report declared that "Jack Turner's avowed resistance to the authorities in 1874, his repeated expressions, in public

36. Atlanta *Constitution,* August 30, 1882; New York *Times,* August 23, 28, 1882.

and private, of bitter, unrelenting hatred to the white
people, his malignity, his turbulence and his revengeful-
ness were well known throughout the county." Thus,
"the recollection of all of Jack's threats, his behavior, the
ardent belief among the people in the existence of the
conspiracy, its diabolical nature so thoroughly in accord
with Jack's nature, the general and widespread feeling of
insecurity so long as the head and front of the conspiracy
lived, so thoroughly outraged and aroused the people
that, under the firm belief of imperious and impending
necessity, they took the law into their own hands, and as
they believed, *to save the lives of many they sacrificed
one.*" [37]

That the plot had existed for so long without discovery
mystified the Selma *Times*. The only explanation seemed
to be the evil genius of the former slave. "Jack Turner,
the conceiver and concoctor of the whole scheme, appears to have been the leaven in the mass, and to have
set to work with an Iago-like craft and fiendishness to
secure the permeation of his devilish hate among the
blacks in his country." The paper could only conclude
that "Vigilance will be more necessary in the future than
in the past." [38] The Butler *Courier* piously remarked that
"If an imperious public necessity ever demanded the
death of one man, that man was Jack Turner. It did not
seem to us to be our duty to imperil or sacrifice a single
family or life in the county except the arch-fiend who
concocted the hellish plot." The people simply could
not afford to wait for an overt act. After all, was it not
true that Jack Turner was one "who, for eight years has
cherished in his heart the desire to outrage and murder

37. Special Citizens' Report.
38. Quoted in Butler *Courier*, August 30, 1882.

an entire county, and whose accidental arrest alone prevented the attempt at its execution?" Why "turn over a second time a criminal of such fiendish propensities and diabolical powers." Was it logical to see him go to jail, serve six short months, and be "released with increased longings to accomplish his hellish designs? If so, the theory of self-protection has been completely obliterated from the code of human laws." [39]

All of the defenders invariably brought up the "Invasion of Butler," but none reported it correctly. The general view, distorted and inaccurate, was that Jack Turner had attempted to invade Butler in 1874 and burn the town. Only the diligence of the whites had prevented the disaster. While making the point that Jack had unsuccessfully tried to reduce Butler to ashes, various writers continued their character analysis. "Those who know him best (white and colored)," the Eutaw *Whig and Observer* explained, "say he was a bold and bad man, and was hated and feared by both white and black." Lynch law might be reprehensible, "yet when the people have cause to believe that their families are to be butchered, in the dead hour of night, by a demon like this man Jack Turner is said to have been," they had to protect themselves. If the Negro were guilty, as he evidently was, then anyone who criticized the Choctaw countians for hanging the conspirator "deserves the same, if not a worse fate, than that of Jack Turner." [40]

One Alabama editor considered the hanging something of a blessing. He explained that Jack Turner "has ruled the negroes of Choctaw with a rod of iron and his death is a relief to them. His taking off has doubtless saved the

39. Butler *Courier*, September 6, 1882.
40. *Ibid.*, quoting Selma *Times*.

life of many of his deluded followers who yielded him an unwilling obedience through fear, and reluctantly lent themselves to his lawless purpose." [41]

Writing as "High Private," Robert McKee offered his own psychoanalysis of Jack Turner. "Who and what was he?" McKee posed rhetorically. "He was a negro, ignorant, turbulent and lawless, whose incendiary conduct has for years been a menace to the people of the county at large, and a curse to his race especially." Bringing in the inevitable reference to the "Invasion of Butler," McKee was no more accurate in his statements than others had been. After the abortive invasion, "High Private" continued: "It was proved then, that Turner was at the head of a semi-military organization, and that his commands were obeyed by his followers as if obedience was an obligation. This organization he appears to have kept up while he lived, and it was with it he meditated a general massacre of the whites at the time he met his doom." Yet if Jack Turner was so evil, the natural question was why did the other blacks follow him? McKee had an answer: "Ignorant and brutal, even for a negro, he still had the capacity to influence others more ignorant and brutal still, to unite with him in absurd and dangerous conspiracies against the public peace, and thus for eight years at least kept a whole county in apprehension." [42]

A number of McKee's contemporaries failed to keep their arguments at a philosophical level. A Tuscaloosa writer who deprecated violence, demanded peace and order, and was willing to grant social and political rights to blacks was unwilling to "hold up to public condemna-

41. Demopolis *News-Journal*, August 26, 1882.
42. "High Private" in Montgomery *Advertiser*, August 31, 1882.

tion any civilized community for ridding itself of a dangerous enemy." [43] Cutting through any troubling second thoughts, a Black Belt paper saw the issue simply: to eliminate the source of the trouble was to eliminate the trouble. "Capt. Jack Turner, who got his deserts from Judge Lynch's court, was the ringleader in the diabolical scheme to murder the white people of the county." His beneficial death had aborted a revolution and rid the county of a sinister character.[44] No commentator revealed himself more openly than one in east Alabama who wrote, "In this case, we think the penalty of the law was not commensurate with the crime. Hanging itself is too good for such a fiend incarnate." [45]

Writer after writer and speaker after speaker took up the theme that Jack Turner deserved to die. A Democratic brochure spoke of him as a turbulent and violent man, denouncing his vicious moral character and his wicked disposition. An unnamed member of his own race was quoted as saying that even if Jack were innocent of the conspiracy charge, he was fully capable of it, and should have been hanged by the Negroes themselves long ago.[46]

Jack Turner's mesmeric power never failed to elicit comment. "Nor do we forget," the Montgomery *Advertiser* reminded its readers, "that throughout the years of his race rule in Choctaw, he has had the mob at his beck and call, ready to do his bidding and carry out his evil designs without reckoning of the consequences." [47] The New York *Herald* had a special correspondent report on

43. Tuskaloosa *Gazette*, September 7, 1882.
44. Greensboro *Alabama Beacon*, September 1, 1882.
45. Opelika *Times*, August 25, 1882.
46. Special Election Pamphlet.
47. Montgomery *Advertiser*, August 31, 1882.

the situation in Alabama. The Northern paper's journalist seconded former reports about Jack Turner, concluding, "It was the well-known dangerous character of the man which rendered the whites ready to believe any evidence of a conspiracy headed by him and which resulted in his death." [48] In their strictures on the Negro leader, the critics never doubted his intelligence. Yet in their haste to condemn him, they revealed a serious flaw in their case. As one of the Negro's defenders wrote, "Nothing could be clearer than that such a man as Jack Turner is represented as being, would not be the fool to organize a conspiracy and put all the details on paper, over and over again. It is entirely inconsistent with the character given the man." [49]

As the November election approached, the intensity of the controversy increased. A black man in Choctaw County was dead. Regardless of the justifications—ranging from the broad critique of the Black Everyman, to the defense of the home (with ramifications), to the authenticity of the documents (with amplifications), to politics, to the uncontrollable propensity for evil inside Jack Turner—the act of offering them (or of being forced to offer them) focused attention on the event and the man.

Having moved from slave to freedman and from tenant farmer to landowning yeoman, Jack Turner was no longer a local leader in an obscure part of a Deep South state. At Tuscahoma, Mount Sterling, Butler, Bladon Springs, and other communities in the county his fol-

48. Quoted in Mobile *Daily Register*, November 3, 1882. The reporter apparently did not consult with any blacks, and while he missed several important points, his dispatch contained valuable insights into Alabama's political situation.
49. Hartford *Courant*, August 31, 1882.

lowers felt the loss of a leader. Chloe and the children went through the motions of keeping themselves together as a family and began a determined struggle to hold on to their land. As the details of Jack's death became known, many people who had never heard of the man came to admire his indomitable courage. His example fired the imagination of black people and numerous white Southerners and Northerners appalled by the death of a brave man. In Alabama the name Jack Turner became central to the furious political battles that raged across the state.

7

The Election

THE FALL OF 1882 seemed like any other fall in Choctaw County. Clumps of sassafras trees along fencerows
turned orange-red, and the leaves from sweetgums—
yellow, dark purple, red—floated quietly to the earth.
Brown-seared stalks of corn stood haphazard sentry in
the fields. Across the county, cotton gins hummed with
activity, and soon it would be time to grind the cane
and savor the taste of new syrup. After the autumn frosts
would come the hard freezes and hog-killing would begin.

For congressional candidates Thomas H. Herndon and
Luther R. Smith it was a desperate season. For the accused conspirators it was a time of anxiety, and for Chloe
and the children, it was a bitter and lonely time. As the
political campaign unfolded, the expected positions were
taken, the expected pronouncements were made, but
overriding all of the issues and never forgotten, whether
mentioned or not, was the hanging of Jack Turner. His
death changed the campaign from a routine victory by
Bourbons expressing the usual platitudes about the Lost
Cause and pledging allegiance to economy in government, into one of fundamental soul baring. The Turner

issue would soon become important in areas other than the First District.

Judge Smith proved himself to be an able campaigner. His strategy, simple in design but difficult to execute, was to appeal to as many white voters as possible. More important, he had to persuade the black voters to turn out in large numbers on election day. Smith and other Republicans hoped that the resentment and hurt following the hanging of Jack Turner would find emphatic expression at the polls. As one writer asserted, "The blood of Jack Turner cries from the ground, and in his grave he will be a greater power against the Bourbons of the south than he ever could have become if left alive and unmolested." [1]

The coalition of Republicans, Greenbackers, and Independents (with the aid of certain outside journalists) built a strong case that the hanging had been an act of political murder. As one writer pointed out, Jack had been the leader of the blacks in Choctaw County. As chairman of the Republican county executive committee and as a delegate to the district convention, he had led his party to victory in the August elections. His death meant the elimination of a powerful opponent to the Democrats.[2] "Jack Turner," a Northern reporter commented, "was obnoxious on account of his meddling with politics." [3]

The hanging could also serve to intimidate other blacks from voting. "It only requires a very few hangings and whippings," a Washington newspaper remarked, "to 'make the nigger keep his place' in election time. And

1. Hartford *Courant*, August 31, 1882.
2. New York *Tribune*, August 25, 1882.
3. Hartford *Courant*, September 16, 1882.

these are the tactics of the so-called 'wealth and intelligence' which we are told will not submit to negro domination." [4] Denying any plot by the blacks, the Hartford *Courant* added, "But on the other hand, knowing the ways of the southern democrat in places where the negro vote is in the majority, there is every reason for believing that the conspiracy business was deliberately cooked up for the purpose of inaugurating a reign of terror, which would suffice to keep the negro from the polls." [5] In citing Jack's services to his party, including his role in testifying about Democratic violations of elections laws, the Arthur Republican Club in Mobile did not doubt that his hanging was intended to serve as a warning to other blacks.[6]

George Turner saw a close connection between the lynching and politics. He said that Jack Turner's leadership "and his activity and success in driving the Bourbons so close at the election induced bad and malicious men to desire to get rid of him." [7] Philip Joseph agreed in his Mobile *Gazette* that the murder was political, but he did not believe the strategy would work. "Jack Turner is now a martyr, whose name will be the rallying cry of republicans all over the north and west. The cowardly act of the Choctaw county democrats will not only unite the republicans of other states, but will unite the opposition to democracy in the first congressional district of Alabama." [8]

4. Montgomery *Advertiser*, September 27, 1882, quoting Washington *Republican*.

5. Hartford *Courant*, August 26, 1882. For a similar editorial see *ibid.*, August 24, 1882.

6. Resolution quoted in Montgomery *Advertiser*, August 31, 1882.

7. Interview with George Turner in New York *Times*, August 26, 1882.

8. Quoted in Butler *Courier*, September 6, 1882.

In the opinion of the New York *Times* the black man's forceful role had made him a "marked man," and his death would serve to "strike terror into the hearts of the negro voters and insure the usual Democratic majority." In sober and unmistakable words the *Times* declared, "There is evidence of a distinct purpose in every part of this affair. The murder of JACK TURNER was apparently deliberately planned and deliberately carried out for a political purpose." [9] A Midwestern Republican editor concurred. He believed that the hanging was political, calculated to aid the Democrats, and would open a season of violence in Alabama. The Bourbons were in an enviable position. "With a jail full of negroes they can run one out and hang him every few days, and thus get up a slate of terrorism which they hope may keep the colored people away from voting." [10]

The Democrats geared their campaign toward denying that the hanging was political and asserting that the Republicans were attempting to make it so. They also effectively exploited the theme that Choctaw County, the state of Alabama, and the South were being mercilessly persecuted and harangued by Yankee editors ignorant of the real state of affairs. Judge Smith was attacked as a base betrayer of his race, a man friendly with the infamous Jack Turner, and a threat to the preservation of white supremacy. Finally, what began as timorous statements and muted innuendoes—suggestions that the plot in Choctaw County was not only real but extended throughout the First District—became open assertions. The rallying of white voters to protect themselves against some unnamed, unspeakable black conspiracy worked so

9. New York *Times,* August 28, 1882.
10. Chicago *Inter Ocean,* August 25, 1882, quoting a telegram from Washington, D.C.

effectively that it was employed in other Alabama congressional contests and became a unique political phenomenon known as "Jack Turnerism." It was easy to point out that the "fact" of Jack Turnerism in the First District made undeniable the "potential" of similar occurrences in other districts. Jack became an effective instrument to assure white solidarity.

"The Northern Republican press, true to their habit of slandering the South, have taken up the Choctaw conspiracy affair." [11] Thus did one Greensboro journalist express his displeasure. Interference from north of the Mason and Dixon line drew a typical response from the Montgomery *Advertiser:* "We don't approve the lynching ourselves, but it don't [*sic*] make any difference to us what the northern Republican press thinks of the matter. We have got along with the negroes in spite of the best efforts of these papers to stir up strife. It is a matter that concerns us, and we propose to do the best we can in our own way to solve this question. All condemnation and abuse from the northern press on a matter it knows nothing about is a gratuitous insult to a people it has slandered through a long series of years." [12]

A Black Belt editor felt that hanging Jack Turner had been a mistake not because of any moral or ethical considerations but because the event had given Northern journals an opportunity to attack the South.[13] Affecting a gentle approach, a Louisiana writer explained to people in other regions that the case had been one where a group of ignorant Negroes had been duped by a shrewd leader. After all, "The bloody shirt is such a ragged,

11. Greensboro *Alabama Beacon,* September 8, 1882.
12. Montgomery *Advertiser,* August 30, 1882.
13. Linden *Reporter,* September 1, 1882, quoting Mobile *Item.*

beggarly garment now, that this affair will scarcely produce much excitement North." When blacks were tricked
"into wild communistic ideas," the scheme usually wound
up, "as this affair did, in a lynching party." [14]

Without question Southern newspapers had adroitly
turned Northern criticism to the advantage of the Democratic party. A New York reporter interpreted the situation: "The report, industriously circulated, that the
Northern Republican press was vilifying the whole people
of the State and of the South on account of this lynching in an obscure portion of Alabama, has had an effect
in rousing popular feeling and turning the current of
popular thought into the old anti-negro channel." [15]

As for the hanging's political implications, most Alabama newspapers and politicians declared that it had
none. In fact, Choctaw County officials announced that
politics had actually protected Jack. Had he not been a
Republican he would have long since been killed through
individual violence.[16] Even so, Robert McKee admitted
that the Democratic party was being damaged by the
reaction.[17] To offset any permanent disadvantage, the
Bourbons moved to demonstrate that to the extent the
hanging was politically motivated, those involved had
been Republicans. They also moved to force Judge Smith

14. New Orleans *Times-Democrat,* August 22, 1882.

15. Mobile *Register,* November 3, 1882, quoting New York *Herald.*

16. Special Citizens' Report. See also Montgomery *Advertiser,* August 31, 1882; Mobile *Daily Register,* September 10, 1882. The Hayneville *Examiner,* September 6, 1882, noting that Jack "took a full hand in politics," equated this with his "devilish conduct."

17. See Robert McKee as "High Private" in Montgomery *Advertiser,* August 31, 1882; and Robert McKee to R. W. Cobb, September 14, 1882, Governor Rufus W. Cobb's Book, June 1882–November 1882, pp. 302–303.

to affirm or deny that political intrigue had caused the death of Jack Turner.

"The carpet-bagger and scalawag are morally responsible for every race trouble in the South," was the firm conviction of one Choctaw countian.[18] Another Democrat reasoned that the Republican-Greenbacker coalition, knowing it had no hope of victory, *wanted* the hanging to occur and provide an election issue. The episode had been concocted in the North and probably devised by George Turner.[19] People who connected politics with the hanging were merely seeking to make electioneering capital. It was far more likely, a Talladega editor wrote, that certain parties provoked the incident knowing that its results would "furnish grist to the outrage mill." [20]

The attack on Judge Smith became highly personal. Voters were told, "If you want to kill Republicanism in Choctaw county, now is the time to deal the death blow. . . . L. R. Smith is their trump card, and defeat in this election means death to republicanism in this district." [21] A report from a Livingston newspaper that during the August campaign "Lucifer Radical Smith" and Jack Turner had been seen canvassing the district together was picked up by other Bourbon journals and offered as evidence that Smith favored social equality.[22] In an editorial entitled "Birds Of A Feather," the Mobile

18. Butler *Courier*, September 6, 1882.
19. Tuskaloosa *Gazette*, September 7, 1882. For a similar view see *ibid.*, August 24, 1882, quoting Meridian *Mercury*.
20. Talladega *Our Mountain Home*, September 6, 1882. In agreement, the Atlanta *Constitution*, absolving the blacks, declared that the affair was manufactured "by white republicans—a class that has betrayed an extreme hatred of negroes recently." See issue of August 22, 1882.
21. Butler *Courier*, October 21, 1882.
22. Demopolis *Marengo News-Journal*, September 6, 1882, quoting Livingston *Journal*. See also Butler *Courier*, October 7, 1882.

Daily Register commented on the incident. The paper was horrified that Smith was the kind of Republican "some white citizens of Mobile, claiming respectability, propose to vote for." [23]

Smith's campaign coffers were extremely limited, and at one point he received a cash donation from Republican party officials in Washington. There was some confusion about how the money was to be disbursed and spent, but the matter was settled after Smith went to Mobile and conferred with party leaders, including blacks. The caviling Butler *Courier* quickly seized the issue as an example of Smith's capitulation and degradation before Negroes. "This little episode has reduced Smith 100 degrees in our estimation," Editor Heyward Taylor wrote. "Heretofore we looked upon him as an erring but dignified political aspirant. Now we know him as a time-serving, degraded carpet-bagger, willing to accept office from a negro constituency. . . . The white man who would submit to be summoned by a few negro politicians and made to render an account of his stewardship, and *eat his own words,* is a stigma on his color, and is beneath the respect of the blackest and most ignorant negro in the United States." Thus did the "high and mighty ruler of the negroes in Choctaw, and the intimate and sworn friend of the Exalted Jack Turner" fall on his knees before the blacks.[24]

Amid the barrage of attacks on the Republican candidate,[25] the Mobile *Daily Register* exploited an issue

23. Mobile *Daily Register,* September 20, 1882. For a denial of the incident see Livingston *Journal,* September 29, 1882.

24. Butler *Courier,* October 14, 1882.

25. For typical attacks on Smith's integrity see Demopolis *Marengo News-Journal,* September 9, 1882; Butler *Courier,* October 24, 1882; Special Election Pamphlet.

that seemed certain to defeat him. If Smith should state that Jack Turner's hanging was political, then all white voters would be alienated. If Smith denied that the lynching had political connotations, the blacks would drop their support. At the very least the former jurist could be made to appear as a recreant hypocrite. After a Mississippi paper quoted Smith as saying the hanging was nonpolitical, the Arthur Club in Mobile asked for an accounting. Smith went to Mobile and satisfactorily denied the remarks attributed to him. While there he was interviewed by the *Register* and pressed to give an answer. Asked if he thought the hanging was politically inspired, Smith replied that he had been out of the county when the event occurred, adding that "your people here, in Mobile, and all over the State, know what it was done for. You know as well, or better, than I can tell." [26] No doubt the puzzled reporter departed, feeling somehow (and correctly) that he had been bested in the interview.

But the *Daily Register* did not give up so easily. Members of the paper's staff wrote to citizens in Choctaw County asking if they remembered what Judge Smith had said about the hanging. One reply came jointly from A. Abney and Oliver C. Ulmer (who added the name of another prominent white man, C. A. Spangenberg). The men reported a conversation they had with Smith on September 14. They reminded him that he had been nominated by a Republican convention that had also passed a resolution condemning the political hanging. Judge Smith supposedly said "certainly" when asked if he knew that Democrats, Greenbackers, and Republicans

26. Mobile *Daily Register,* October 4, 1882. See also Livingston *Journal,* October 6, 1882.

had participated in the hanging and that there was nothing political about it.[27]

S. Croom was another Choctaw countian who responded to the *Daily Register*'s query. Croom reported that on September 3, he and the judge had both been on board the steamer *Ruth* bound for Mobile. At that time Smith postulated that the hanging had occurred because the people believed a conspiracy existed. George H. Carnathan (prominent young lawyer who had earned his degree at the University of Alabama and son of William G. Carnathan, the planter involved in the election controversy of 1880) also wrote the paper. Not yet twenty-five, the barrister served as solicitor in 1880, and probably had encounted Turner in election disputes. Shortly after Smith was nominated he and Carnathan had a conversation. The Republican said he had heard that Carnathan was not at the hanging. "I told him I was not." Smith asked why. "I told him I was unavoidably kept away; that I was very sorry I was not there; and that if I had been, I would have been in favor of hanging the balance of the rascals implicated. I told him I had not attended the meeting held by the citizens, for the reason that I had personal feelings against Jack Turner, and thought my actions might be misconstrued." Smith remarked that Carnathan had behaved properly. "I then said: Judge, I suppose the 'Rads' will try to make a great political howl out of the hanging of Jack." Smith responded, "They ought not, as politics had nothing to do with it." [28]

27. Letter quoted in Mobile *Daily Register,* October 10, 1882.
28. *Ibid.* For a sketch of Carnathan see Owen, *History of Alabama and Dictonary of Alabama Biography,* III, 301.

The Bourbons did not let up. If Judge Smith's personal life and character were abused, the more general menace of a return to the corrupt days of Republican hegemony was not neglected. If the vilification of Jack Turner as a subspecies of man continued, the threat that his race posed to white supremacy was widely proclaimed. If a white man voted Republican, then he approved of Jack Turner, and to approve of Jack Turner was to deny Caucasian rule. Even Robert McKee wrote, "That [Jack Turner] was a leader of the Republican party in his county, and a member of the Republican district committee, are facts which tend to fix the character of that party in the State." [29]

"The Voice of the Carpetbagger is now heard again in the land," a Democratic brochure warned the voters. "His language and his methods are the same as in 1868. In the Convention which nominated Judge Smith the hanging of Jack Turner in Choctaw county was seized upon with fiendish delight as a pretext for firing the heart of the misguided African and setting him at enmity with his white fellow-citizens." All of this was done even though "Jack Turner was a turbulent and violent negro, into whose heart the white Radicals had breathed a hatred of our people which he manifested in a thousand ways. . . . Yet this bad man was declared a martyr by the Republican Convention at Mobile." Without mincing words, the pamphlet concluded, "Citizens! rouse yourselves to ward off the desperate efforts now being made to revive the rule of the Radicals in this land, and to take us backward to the dark days of 1868. Let it plainly appear that when the attempt is made, *as it now is,* to give political ascendency to the negro, the white man

29. "High Private" to Montgomery *Advertiser,* August 31, 1882.

will maintain his own superior claim to the control of public affairs." [30]

"Jack Turnerism" became a phrase used to describe the strangest aspect of the political campaign. The Mobile *Daily Register* set the stage by suggesting that certain blacks who had been involved in the Jack Turner conspiracy were actively promoting Smith's candidacy. Their activities, instigated by the Radicals, had the effect of stirring up the blacks against the whites. The paper mentioned secret meetings of blacks in Mobile, Clarke, and Choctaw counties. They were conducted "by men who disappeared from their homes immediately after the execution of Jack Turner." Now scattered across the First Congressional District—Washington, Choctaw, Marengo, Clarke, Monroe, and Mobile counties—they were sowing the seeds of further trouble, luring innocent Negroes into the meshes of secret societies. The *Daily Register* wanted whites to hold public meetings in every beat and suggested that leading white citizens should make speeches to blacks counteracting the designs of unscrupulous agitators. All of the evidence pointed to unrest among the Negroes. "Agents of persons having ends to subserve are stealthily moving from one neighborhood to another, holding meetings to which colored people only are admitted, and over which sentinels are posted, and at the door of which passwords are used for admittance." [31]

Was there any evidence to support the claims of a widespread conspiracy? In the First District, Choctaw

30. Special Election Pamphlet. See also Grove Hill *Clarke County Democrat,* September 14, 1882.
31. Mobile *Daily Register,* September 2, 1882. See also Gainesville *Reporter,* September 7, 1882.

County was the supreme example, but other counties were also mentioned. Whites living in the Kempville neighborhood in Monroe County reported that Negroes were holding secret midnight conclaves. Coming in the wake of the Jack Turner episode, the gatherings alarmed the whites who demanded that the blacks explain their activities.[32] "What do they want?" a white citizen asked. "Have they other JACK TURNERS to sacrifice upon the altar of colored folly, colored ambition and colored hate?" [33]

A Black Belt citizen reasoned that a Negro conspiracy could not be confined to one county alone. In antebellum times the ignorant blacks had attempted sporadic, isolated uprisings, but it was plain "that the colored race *now* are too well-informed and well-posted to believe they could conquer and hold just a single county in a populous State like Alabama." Did this mean that the plot in Choctaw County was patently ridiculous? Just the opposite. Daily news reports from other parts of the state were startling, and "the evidence is conclusive that the murderous plot was not confined to Choctaw alone, but is or was widespread, and if it all should really come to light, is perhaps co-extensive with the whole State." In short, "*The Choctaw people were right*—the plot *was* a *bona fide* and murderous conspiracy!—the senseless howling and raving of Radical fanatics and capital-makers to the contrary notwithstanding." [34]

The Democrats now had the perfect issue. They had parlayed Jack Turner's supposed massacre of the whites

---

32. Mobile *Daily Register,* September 21, 1882, quoting Monroeville *Monroe Journal.*
33. Grove Hill *Clarke County Democrat,* September 7, 1882.
34. Carrollton *West Alabamian,* September 20, 1882.

from a maniacal act of revenge into a political conspiracy intended to gain control of Choctaw County. His deluded followers, even now, were busy plotting to seize the machinery of government throughout the First District. The Bourbon strategy seemed to be working so well that it became desirable to use it in other districts where the Democrats faced challenges at the polls. To this end, one editor noted that in southern and southeast Alabama (in the Second and Third districts) there were ominous stirrings, there was "something wrong among portions of the colored people." [35]

The most widespread reports of Negro conspiracies occurred in the Second District made up of Butler, Crenshaw, Pike, Conecuh, Covington, and Escambia counties. In Butler County one "Little John" White, short of statue and approximately thirty years old, appeared about the time of the difficulties in Choctaw County. For a time "Little John" was confused with Jack Turner, but in any case, the Negro was active in the Pine Flat neighborhood. He wore a blue uniform with stripes on his coat sleeves and collar, and he was further distinguished by a strand of beads around his neck. "Little John" proclaimed himself a United States Marshal with authority to lead the blacks against the whites. Preaching at a Negro church near Pine Flat, he commanded his black audience either to kill the whites or leave the country. White had with him pistols and handcuffs to be used in making personal arrests. The strange minister-lawman also advised the Negroes to engage in a massive work stoppage. The only difficulty with the story was its source: it emanated from a single white man who was convinced of the demoralizing effect of

35. Greensboro *Alabama Beacon,* September 22, 1882.

White's visitation. There was, in fact, no work stoppage, no mass migration, and no hint of an uprising. As for "Little John," he allegedly escaped before he could be arrested. Despite its falsity, the story was circulated by the state press as an example of "Jack Turnerism" and alarmed many whites.[36]

From Escambia County the Brewton *Blade* reported the formation of an insurrectionary organization of blacks that was arming Negroes and preparing to exterminate the whites. The paper was worried that the entire territory was "contaminated by these blood-thirsty incendiaries." [37] The same organization was supposedly active in Conecuh and Covington counties. Early in September incriminating documents were discovered that outlined an insurrection at Burnt Corn in Conecuh County. After considerable excitement four of the ringleaders were placed under arrest. There were also a number of arrests made in Covington County.[38] But, as in Butler County, there was no revolt. The stories had no basis in fact, although they were reprinted (complete with worried editorials) in many Alabama newspapers.

The whites became so apprehensive that any gathering of blacks made them suspicious. After rumors were circulated at Helicon in Crenshaw County about a militant Negro holding meetings of blacks, the white citizens held one themselves. The situation had become so tense they "*Resolved,* That the negroes of this community be re-

---

36. Carrollton *West Alabamian,* September 20, 1882, quoting Greensville *Advocate;* see also Mobile *Daily Register,* September 10, 1882; Montgomery *Advertiser,* September 13, 1882.

37. Quoted in Carrollton *West Alabamian*, September 20, 1882.

38. Mobile *Daily Register,* September 10, 1882, quoting Evergreen *News* and Evergreen *Conecuh Star;* Montgomery *Advertiser,* September 9, 1882; Carrollton *West Alabamian,* September 20, 1882.

quested to remain quietly at home, as any gathering or demonstration by them might be construed or looked upon as a furtherance of designs inimical to the peace and welfare of this people." [39]

Henry, a wiregrass county in the Third District, was the locale of yet another racial disturbance. There a Negro schoolteacher supposedly attracted a large following by preaching insurrectionary doctrine. The false prophet escaped before a warrant issued for his arrest could be served.[40]

About this time a Negro identifying himself as Monroe White (some thought he was "Little John" White of Butler County fame) began making speeches in the Washington precinct of Autauga County. Of small size and wearing a uniform of mixed pattern with stripes down his pants, Monroe White informed his listeners in the Fifth District that he had been dispatched from Washington and had credentials supplied by President Arthur. In his fiery speeches, Monroe White urged black women not to wash clothes for white people for less than a dollar a day. He promised that cotton would increase in price to thirty-five cents a pound, while meat would go down to four cents a pound. President Arthur and General Grant, his listeners were assured, would soon order troops into the South. In a few months social equality would be established; whites and Negroes would eat and sleep together and intermarry. Moreover, on September 15, "six feet of dirt" would be presented free to every Negro voter who failed to renounce the Demo-

39. Montgomery *Advertiser*, September 17, 1882, quoting Troy *Messenger*. The same black was also reported in Pike County.
40. Carrollton *West Alabamian*, September 20, 1882, quoting Eufaula *Bulletin*.

cratic party. Whites who attempted to interfere would be summarily dealt with. Not unexpectedly, White was arrested for his efforts. He supposedly "confessed" that he had been hired by Republican leaders—the list included everybody from George Turner to Senator Roscoe Conkling of New York—to go about the countryside stirring up trouble.[41] George Turner angrily denied that he or other Republicans had any connections with Monroe White and suggested that either White was demented or the Democrats themselves had brazenly contrived the bogus charges.[42]

The "Red Man" of Shelby County was the most bizarre example of "Jack Turnerism." Known also as Mercy Carr or Muscarcar (apparently his real name was Mercer Kerr), the Red Man was outrageously costumed: he wore red pants with white stripes, a red shirt, a long buff coat trimmed at the sleeves with red flannel and sewed in various places with crosses; a red skull cap emblazoned with a yellow cross; and over it all, a yellow gown. People in the Seventh District had never seen anything like the Red Man who claimed, among other things, that he was a Catholic priest. The Red Man, a native of Tennessee but long since moved North, handed out a message strikingly similar to that of Monroe White. Shelby blacks were promised three hundred dollars with which to purchase arms. Since the land was rightfully theirs, Negroes were urged by the Red Man to kill the whites and take it. Black women had been too long at the

41. Montgomery *Advertiser*, September 13, 1882; Carrollton *West Alabamian*, September 20, 1882, quoting Prattville *Signal*.
42. See George Turner's telegram to Montgomery *Advertiser*, September 26, 1882.

washtubs of white women. Liberation for the colored people would come with aid from Northern whites and General William T. Sherman's army. The Red Man was not allowed to make many speeches before being arrested and placed in jail at Columbiana.[43]

A few rational citizens prevented an extremely edgy populace from hanging the Red Man. Even though he was a Democrat, an editor in a neighboring county could not resist a taunt: "We are glad to see that the people of Shelby appealed to the law and not to Judge Lynch as did the people of Choctaw, to the great detriment of the good character of the State for law and order." [44] It later turned out that the black had traveled with a circus, and that before leaving it had acquired his colorful wardrobe. A Negro editor was no doubt correct in dismissing the antics of the Red Man as those of an unbalanced individual.[45]

Other counties where black plots were reported included Baldwin, Calhoun, Lee, Washington, Lowndes, Talladega, and Wilcox. What did all of these stories mean and what was their significance? The Montgomery *Advertiser* advised moderation and great caution on the part of the people. "Let them keep their eyes open and have the parties guilty of violating the laws arrested and lodged in jail." [46] The general interpretation by Democrats was that the blacks were attempting to revert to

43. Mobile *Daily Register,* September 5, 1882, quoting Columbiana *Shelby Sentinel;* see also Montgomery *Advertiser,* September 2, 1882; Camden *News and Pacificator,* October 6, 1882.

44. Six Mile *Bibb Blade,* August 31, 1882.

45. Huntsville *Gazette,* September 30, 1882. See also Hartford *Courant,* October 4, 1882, quoting Tuskegee *Macon Mail.*

46. Montgomery *Advertiser,* September 9, 1882. See *ibid.,* September 5, 1882.

the troubled days of the Union League, usually called the Loyal League, and that their efforts were a serious menace to the white race.[47]

In Connecticut, Joseph R. Hawley's Hartford *Courant* viewed Democratic stories of evil blacks assembled in secret societies as attempts to frighten whites and as "evidence of an intention to suppress the colored vote at any cost." [48] The Washington *Republican* credited the ever-inventive Bourbons with a new device. They hired a black and had him "perambulate in Alabama as a fiery destroyer of white men. He delivered speeches on the stump, informing the crowd that he is fomenting a bloody massacre. . . . Then come Bourbon reports of the mighty secrets he divulged." It seemed certain "that the Bourbons fear the effect of a full Republican vote in the black belt, and that they are reviving the old time policy of intimidation, and violence when necessary." [49]

Robert McKee, despite his attempts to rectify his critical letter to Choctaw County officials and take the political sting out of the hanging, was far too rational a man to put credence in the stories of a general Negro uprising. He wrote to L. W. Grant of the Jacksonville *Republican* congratulating him on his well-reasoned editorials. The private secretary agreed that the hysteria was senseless. After all, McKee argued, within recent memory the Loyal Leagues had met long and often, and for that matter, blacks had the legal right to assemble. "Our women and children were not afraid of the negroes during the war, when there were motives to revolt, and when there was

47. Special Election Pamphlet; Mobile *Daily Register,* September 17, 1882.
48. Hartford *Courant,* September 7, 1882.
49. Quoted in Montgomery *Advertiser,* September 27, 1882.

reason to fear that federal emissaries were exciting them
to it; and it looks a little strange to see men who for four
years faced the perils of a great war now panic-stricken
by such negro meetings as were held everywhere and
every week a few years ago, magnified by idle rumor
into strategems, conspiracy, and treason. . . . It is only
to be regretted that [your articles were] not written
months ago." [50]

"Jack Turnerism" was an important factor in the campaign. The horrific reaction of newspaper editors undoubtedly aided the Bourbons. Many readers, inclined
to accept whatever appeared in their newspapers as the
truth revealed, became convinced that their physical security depended on electing Democrats to office. To be
fair, there were journalists who sincerely believed that
a statewide black conspiracy existed, but most knew
better. There was no plot, and exploiting the threat of
one to gain political advantage assured at least the aggravation of racial animosity and ran the graver risk of pro-
voking actual violence.

No one conversant with politics in Alabama doubted
the results of the election. In all of the congressional districts the Democrats swept to substantial victories. The
bitterly contested race in the First District saw Herndon
defeat Smith but by margins that were disappointing to
Bourbons hopeful of a smashing triumph. The Butler
Courier, which had filled its columns with invective
against Smith, could not be faulted for lack of effort.
"Canvassing the county in Jack Turner's company, and
associating himself with the negroes in denouncing the
white people of this country, are true indexes to his

50. Robert McKee to L. W. Grant, October 22, 1882, Robert
McKee Papers, Alabama Department of Archives and History.

character," the paper asserted. "He is a negro at heart and his white skin should no longer protect him from the treatment given his close associates." [51] The historic fear of slave revolts, the bitterness of Reconstruction, and the Jack Turner affair were used to trigger a highly emotional response, a response carefully channeled into political action. But while triumphant elsewhere, Democratic strategy had only qualified success in Choctaw County and the First District.

Choctaw County had eighteen precincts, each presided over on election day by three inspectors, and a returning officer. The seventy-two officials were all appointed. No black returning officers had been selected, but there were ten Negro inspectors.[52] All day long on Tuesday, November 14, the voters filed past the ballot boxes and cast their votes. Election officials were several days counting the ballots, although a terse preliminary report from Bladon Springs (Precinct No. 14) gave Herndon a majority with "many negroes not voting." [53] The final vote in Choctaw County listed Herndon as defeating Smith 1,278 to 953, a majority of 225 votes. Herndon received solid majorities in Marengo and Washington counties and carried Monroe by 607 votes, but Smith came within 310 votes of victory in Clarke, and only lost populous Mobile County by 457 votes.[54]

It seems probable that a number of Negroes were too intimidated to vote, while numerous whites who might normally have passed up the election were frightened

51. Linden *Reporter,* September 22, 1882, quoting Butler *Courier.*
52. For a precinct breakdown see Butler *Courier,* October 21, 1882.
53. Mobile *Daily Register,* November 10, 1882.
54. Official Election Returns, First District Congressional Contest 1882.

enough to cast their ballots. Yet the results in Choctaw County and throughout the district reveal that the blacks voted, and voted in large numbers. Jack Turner's Choctaw County followers remained loyal, and their example inspired blacks in other counties. Withstanding pressure and coercion, they did not falter in their support of Judge Smith, who deserves credit for waging an intelligent campaign free of the demagogic rhetoric that was employed against him. Herndon's expected runaway victory was thwarted because the blacks, moved at least to a large degree by their determination to express their revulsion at the lynching of Jack Turner, turned out to vote. A small number of whites also voted for the coalition candidate, an act that infuriated Editor Taylor of the Butler *Courier*. He threatened to publish the names of whites who voted for Smith so that they might be revealed as men "who were so blind to their own interests, and false to their lineage as to cast a vote for the negro candidate." [55]

With the election out of the way, the people in Choctaw County became interested in the case against the accused conspirators. What would become of them?

55. Butler *Courier*, November 11, 1882. See Livingston *Journal*, November 17, 1882, for the claim that Smith did not get twenty white votes in Choctaw County. For praise of Smith as a campaigner see the Democratic Grove Hill *Clarke County Democrat*, October 26, 1882.

8

The Last Phase

FRED BARNEY, Aaron Scott, Range West, Willis Lyman, Peter Hill, and Jesse Wilson were successful in getting their case transferred from the county court to the circuit court. As a result of the appeal, they were at least assured of a jury trial even if the grand jury found a true bill against them. Courthouse officials worked overtime in late August issuing subpoenas to witnesses commanding their presence before the grand jury.[1] The defendants, except for Jesse Wilson who evidently raised the one-thousand-dollar bond and was released September 2, were forced to remain in jail.[2]

No one was sure how many witnesses were called, but at least forty-one testified,[3] and on October 21, 1882, the all-white grand jury returned a true bill. According to the indictment, the accused men "wickedly devising and

1. A record of the various subpoenas issued is on file at the Choctaw County Circuit Clerk's Office.
2. See Sheriff's Account for Dieting Prisoners, Choctaw County, July 1, 1882–[——] 4, Circuit Clerk's Office.
3. Choctaw County Grand Jury Proceedings, Fall, 1882, and Spring, 1883, pp. 100–13.

intending to commit murder, fraudulently, maliciously, unlawfully did conspire, confederate, combine, and agree together, between and amongst themselves, [by] force and arms, unlawfully and with malice aforethought to kill certain persons to wit, certain white people in the County of Choctaw whose names are to the Grand Jury unknown." [4]

The grand jury indicted Mose Turner, Zack Ward, and Jim Roberts along with the original defendants. Then in November the name of Little John Keeton, a Negro whose name like those of Turner, Ward, and Roberts was mentioned several times in the grand jury hearing, was added to the list of conspirators. Keeton was not formally arrested until December 8, while Roberts was not taken into custody until February 10, 1883. For some reason Zack Ward was never arrested, although he remained in Choctaw County and was later listed as a witness for the defendants. Mose Turner escaped to Mobile where he was apprehended on a federal charge of violating timber laws. When the sheriff of Choctaw County, armed with a warrant, arrived in Mobile to arrest Mose, United States District Attorney George M. Duskin refused to surrender him. Since he was being held by formal commitment from the United States Commissioner, Mose Turner did not have to answer the charges levied against him in Choctaw County. The Butler *Courier* fumed that federal officers were "harboring, aiding and abetting a negro charged with a high crime against the state of Alabama to escape from the operations of those laws." Whether Mose was receiving federal protection or not, he was never tried in any court:

4. Circuit Court Records, Circuit Clerk's Office.

in October the Negro left Mobile, taking what was referred to as "leg bail."[5]

On October 26, five days after the true bill was returned, J. E. Gray and W. F. Glover, attorneys for the defendants, entered a motion for them to the circuit court asking that a new bond be set. As the lawyers pointed out, the prisoners were unable to raise the one-thousand-dollar bond originally imposed, they had been in jail since their arrests, and their trial would not come up until the spring term. A more reasonable amount would make it possible for them to go free until March.[6] Finally, on December 14, Circuit Judge William E. Clarke set their bail at three hundred dollars each. The amount was still excessive for all of the prisoners except Fred Barney. On December 16, he was bailed.[7] Barney went home to Mount Sterling where his wife Dink and his children were waiting.

Fred Barney had lived a remarkable life. Like his friend Jack Turner he had been a slave. Intellectually gifted, he had acquired an education—perhaps with the aid of the Freedman's Bureau, although it is possible that he learned to read and write while still a bondsman—and become a teacher. Barney's difficulties began when he attempted to apply the promises of Reconstruction outside the classroom. He had become a trusted follower of Jack and was no less dedicated to the goal of achieving a place of dignity in society for himself and his race. The

5. Butler *Courier*, October 14, 1882. For another highly critical account see Mobile *Daily Register*, September 20, 1882. See Sheriff's Dieting Account, 5, 7.

6. Motion Docket, Circuit Court, Choctaw County, Alabama, Commencing With The Fall Term, 1871, Fall Term, 1882, p. 158.

7. Circuit Court Records Choctaw County; Sheriff's Dieting Account, 5.

black pedagogue had fought through political campaigns, patiently taught the young in woefully inadequate schools, and looked after his family. Arrested with the others on conspiracy charges, he had withstood torture and refused to "confess." Then in December, 1882, Fred Barney walked out of jail, temporarily a free man.

But past events caught up with him: he had been arrested, threatened, tortured; his best friend had been lynched; he himself had been indicted and conviction seemed likely. During his confinement the accused man reviewed the course of his existence and apparently concluded that Jack's death had removed the last hope for himself and for the blacks of Choctaw County. Barney developed what were described as symptoms of acute mania. Perhaps for a brief time after his release, the Negro took new hope, but soon the despondency returned. Painful introspection turned into mental torture, and Barney decided that he did not want to remain alive. Neither did he want his children to face the kind of hostile world that he had known. Sometime in January he tried unsuccessfully to kill his children. Breaking down completely, the black teacher attempted to take his own life by drowning, but was pulled from the water. On February 2, 1883, he was rearrested by county authorities. In jail once again, Barney became subdued, detached —sitting for hours without saying a word.[8]

Another of the prisoners, Peter Hill, was suffering from a physical illness described as "consumption" at the

8. Medical Records, State of Alabama Department of Mental Health, Bryce Hospital, Tuscaloosa. Dr. Donald Smith, superintendent of Bryce Hospital, and Dr. Stonewall B. Stickney, state commissioner of Mental health, were both professional and cooperative in making Fred Barney's records available for this study. See also Sheriff's Dieting Account, 7.

time of his arrest. As the weeks became months his condition grew worse. Finally, on February 22, he was released on a one-hundred-dollar bond. In March, Hill died. His death was noted by the *Courier* in a remark callous even for that journal: "Providence has given him a change of venue and an indefinite continuance." [9]

When the circuit court convened in late March, 1883, the prosecution had thirty-seven witnesses. W. F. Glover remained as the defendants' lawyer, although J. E. Gray had been replaced by the recent congressional aspirant, Luther R. Smith. The defense was equally prepared and had called thirty-nine witnesses.[10] The defendants' attorneys—intelligent, experienced, and able—did not suffer in comparison with the state's lawyers. First, Glover and Smith sought to have indictments voided. Their grounds (which undoubtedly set off mutterings of anger within the courtroom) were that the grand jury had been all white. Obviously the men who returned the true bill were not selected from a complete list of householders and residents of the county. The defendants, by the mode of selection of the grand jury alone, had been denied equal protection of the laws.[11] Their motion was denied.

If the victory by the state set off vigorous noddings of approval from the audience, they were of short duration. The defense attorneys quickly asked for a change of venue. They forwarded the irrefutable point that public prejudice against the prisoners made it impossible for them to receive justice in either Choctaw or Marengo counties. Specifically cited were the strictures by the Butler *Courier*. The court ruled that prosecution against

9. Butler *Courier,* March 17, 1883. See also Sheriff's Dieting Account, 7.

10. Choctaw County Circuit Court Records, Book P, 173.

11. *Ibid.,* Spring Term, March 27, 1883

the deceased Peter Hill was to be abated; that as the result of a careful examination in open court it appeared Fred Barney was insane—he was ordered taken to the state hospital for the insane at Tuscaloosa. But what about the others? Where would they stand trial? The court, unmoved by any local pressures, agreed with the defense lawyers. A change of venue was made to Sumter County because "the defendants cannot have a fair and impartial trial in the Counties of Choctaw and Marengo." [12]

The *Courier* reacted as though it had been grievously wronged: "Except as to Jack Turner, who had previously received his deserts, and Mose Turner spirited away by Federal officeholders in Mobile, we made no remarks against any individual suspects; and defy them to show the contrary. Things have reached a pretty pass, when a journalist is arraigned for publishing the names of arrested prisoners; and a statement of the facts leading to their arrest." [13]

Following the change of venue, the prisoners were to be transferred to the jail at Livingston, county seat of Sumter, to await trial before the circuit court. In the second week of April, before the prisoners could be moved, they were all bailed and released.[14] One local white citizen, not surprised at the change of venue, wrote, "While we feel that it is better for the people of Choctaw, that others should try them, we do not think the conspirators themselves will derive much benefit from the change." [15]

12. *Ibid.*, Book D, 1882–83, p. 768.
13. Butler *Courier*, April 7, 1883.
14. Sheriff's Dieting Account, 8; Butler *Courier*, April 14, 1883.
15. Butler *Courier*, April 14, 1883. See also Livingston *Journal*, April 13, 1883.

The indicted men were to be tried at the August term of the circuit court. On May 13 the blacks (and possibly a few whites), ignoring derision, held a ceremony for Jack Turner at Mount Sterling. The meeting amounted almost to a second funeral, only this time there were many in attendance. Turner's name was praised and his innocence declared. Eight months after his death, Negroes realized more than ever his leadership and remembered more than ever how he had died.[16]

The long awaited trial of the accused conspirators, the legal ceremony that would serve, pending conviction, as a vindication of the mob that had hanged Jack Turner, was set for July. Livingston—slightly larger than Butler but similarly laid out around a courthouse square—was the commercial, cultural, and legal center for the Black Belt county of Sumter. During Reconstruction the county had been the scene of considerably more political and racial violence than had Choctaw, and those persons desiring a verdict of guilty had no reason to believe the jurors of Sumter County would be predisposed to find the accused men innocent.

The trial was postponed. Its continuance to the February term, 1884, stemmed from a simple cause: the court docket was so crowded there was not enough time for the case to be heard. "The delay can harm no one," readers of the Butler *Courier* were told, "as the prisoners are under bond and at work." [17]

When February came, those who had braved the cold and accepted the discomforts of the drafty courtroom hoping to see the workings of justice were disappointed.

16. Butler *Courier,* May 12, 1883.
17. *Ibid.,* July 16, 1883. See also Livingston *Journal,* August 3, 1883.

The case was continued once again. The difficulty was a crowded docket and the failure of all the witnesses to appear. In March, 1884, Fred Barney had recovered sufficiently to be released from the hospital. The examining physicians at Tuscaloosa reported him free of physical ailments and diagnosed his mental illness as being caused by the circumstances of the hanging. Barney was rearrested on the conspiracy charge, but remained in jail only one day before friends raised the $150 necessary for bail. At the spring term of the Choctaw County circuit court, Barney sought and was granted a change of venue to Sumter County. No one was surprised when the court, convening at Livingston for its August term, gave the case a continuance until February, 1885.[18]

When the case was called, it turned out that the witnesses, or at least some of them, had not appeared. A new newspaper, the *Choctaw Herald,* one much more temperate in its remarks than Taylor's *Courier,* had been established in Butler. "It does seem that the case could be disposed of in some way and stop the expense of our county," the *Herald*'s editor wrote. "While it may be fun for the officers of the court of Sumter to issue and serve the papers in the case, yet it is quite a burden to the citizens of this county." [19]

In July and August, 1885, new subpoenas were issued and every effort was made to get the witnesses to appear. Although a number made the journey to Livingston, several did not, and the case was assigned the familiar

18. Medical Records, Bryce Hospital, Tuscaloosa; Sheriff's Dieting Account, 15; Appearance Bond for Fred Barney, Circuit Clerk's Office; Butler *Choctaw Herald,* April 3, 1884; Minutes, Sumter County Circuit Court, April, 1880–February, 1885, p. 522, Sumter County Courthouse.

19. *Choctaw Herald,* February 5, 1885.

continuance.[20] After August no one pretended that the prosecution was serious in its intent to have a trial. Passions had cooled in Choctaw County. There had been no further threats from the blacks, and, after all, Jack Turner was dead. No one was uncouth enough to suggest that the lack of vigor in pushing the case lay in the prosecution's fear that it had no case, and that an acquittal would be both embarrassing and damaging to the participants in the lynching—not to mention most of the state press and the Democratic party. Term followed term of the Sumter County court and just as regularly the conspiracy case was continued.[21]

If nothing else, the case took up space on the docket and consumed the court's valuable time. It was clear that the state had no case, and the issue had been in limbo long enough. On October 24, 1887, over five years and two months after Jack Turner was hanged, a final decision was reached. In controlled, graceful script, a cryptic decree was recorded on page 120, Book S, Sumter County circuit court minutes: "It is ordered by the Court that this case be dismissed and the defendants discharged."

People preferred to forget what had happened. No one reminded the citizens of their solemn promises to prove the conspirators guilty and absolve themselves for hanging Jack Turner. The *Choctaw Herald* did not even bother to report the final disposition of the case. Relieved of the prolonged threat of legal action, the defendants were now free men, and, except for Fred Barney who

20. Sumter County Circuit Court, August Term, July 16, August 25, 1885, Circuit Clerk's Office; *Choctaw Herald,* July 23, 1885.
21. Butler *Choctaw Herald,* April 7, 28, 1887; October 27, 1887; Final Record, Sumter County Circuit Court, Book XX, May 1887, p. 59.

resumed his role as a teacher, worked as tenant farmers. Perhaps in the years ahead some of them would become small independent landowners. Like most blacks and whites in the county and across the state, they would struggle against a chronic condition of falling cotton prices and grinding poverty. No matter what the future held for them, burned forever in their consciousness was the shared experience of August 19, 1882, and the following months. And they would always remember the powerful force of Jack Turner.

After Jack's death Chloe Turner fought to hold her land and family. The loss of her husband was a wound that would not heal, but she was not bewildered, and she was resourceful. Somehow, in the next few years she continued to pay taxes on the eighty acres of land (whose evaluation was $100). Finally, the task was overwhelming. In 1889 Chloe was reduced to three head of cattle—fortunately, they were exempt from taxation—and had difficulty paying state and county real estate taxes and a special county tax, all of which amounted to only $1.20.[22] That she held on for almost eight years was a tribute to her indomitable tenacity. In 1890 Chloe was forced to sell all of her land except for six and one-half acres.[23] What happened to her and her children is not known, but it seems likely that the black woman remained in Choctaw County. She had nowhere to go.

Jack Turner's name does not appear in any of the books containing biographies of notable Alabamians. Yet he was an important man. He not only declined to accept the world in which he lived, he attempted to transform

22. Choctaw County Assessment of Taxes on Real Estate and Personal Property, Assessment Records for 1883–89.
23. *Ibid.*, 1890.

it. That he was considered "inferior" did not make him
so. Such status was in the eyes of the beholder, not in the
mind of Jack Turner. Always he was an activist. A society that relegated him and his people to a low level of
citizenship could just as easily elevate them to a place of
equality. He was willing to be and attempted to be the
instrument of change. His individual characteristics made
him a personal (and intolerable) challenge to the status
quo, while his demonstrated ability (equally unaccept-
able) to influence and inspire other blacks to actions—
voting, asserting their rights as citizens—they otherwise
might not have taken, meant an inevitable confrontation
between him and the white rulers. His human weaknesses
were undeniable, but they were hardly extreme. Jack's
whiskey drinking was at once no more pronounced than
that of whites and other blacks and was accomplished no
more or no less as a combination of emotional release and
simple pleasure. Despite his extramarital affair with Eliza
Moseley, it is certain that he loved Chloe and his children
and took care of them. Without doubt his temper, his
consumption of liquor, and certain minor moral foibles
were more than offset by strength and conviction that
would have earned secret if not public admiration for a
white man. The difficulty was that Jack was a black, and
the tendency was to see his assertiveness as "uppityness."

Perhaps the Negro knew in advance that his struggle
would end in defeat, but if so, he was unaffected by such
knowledge. In contesting a system supported by the de-
basement of one race at the expense of another, he forced
the establishment into giving an accounting, into framing
a defense. As the New York *Times* pointed out, the hanging of a Negro in the South was not unheard of. "There
was nothing unusual in that." Hangings were usually re-

ported, accompanied by a few details, and then forgotten. But the lynching of Jack Turner was different. A justification was attempted, and as the *Times* put it, his death was "made the core of an altogether unnecessary myth." [24]

In the years that followed a cloak of silence (more benign than malevolent) fell over the Jack Turner episode. After the bitterness of the initial reaction, whites and blacks, as though by mutual consent, seemed to thrust the deed from their minds and conversation. It was as if the hanging had been too terrible, too agonizing and that the less said about it the better. Decades later when the event was an obscure memory it was discussed and then only on occasion and always in hushed tones. But doubts remained and uncertainties persisted. Did the black leader conspire to massacre the entire white population of Choctaw County, Alabama? Or was his death the result of a deliberate plan to eliminate a political enemy accomplished by a small group of men who cynically manipulated their fellow citizens? The questions now sound merely rhetorical. He was lynched. The complex reasons for the hanging range from the belief by some that he was guilty to personal hatred by others; but if Jack Turner was silenced, his impact on the state is undeniable.

24. New York *Times,* August 23, 1882.

List of Sources

UNPUBLISHED MATERIAL

Alabama Archives and History, Montgomery
    Alabama Census, Agricultural, I, 1850, I, 1860
    Choctaw County Census, Population, 1860, 1870, 1880
    Choctaw County Census, Slave, 1860
    Cobb, Governor Rufus W., Letter Book, June 1882–November, 1882
    Lewis, David P., Governor's Correspondence
    McKee, Robert, Papers
    Official Election Returns:
        First District Congressional Contest, 1882
        Fourth District Congressional Contest, 1872
        Governor's Contest, 1872, 1874, 1880, 1882
    Works Progress Administration (WPA) Manuscripts
Choctaw County Courthouse, Butler (1870–1890)
    Circuit Clerk's Office:
        Appearance Bonds
        Arrest Warrants
        Circuit Court Records

County Court Records
Grand Jury Dockets
Grand Jury Proceedings
Motion Dockets
Sheriff's Accounts of Dieting Prisoners
Probate Judge's Office:
Deed Record, Book N
Inventories, Book C
Last Will and Testament of B. L. Turner
Marriage Records, Colored, Book 1
Mortgage Records, Books S, T, U, V, and W
Registration Book, 1875
Tax Assessor's Office:
Assessment of Taxes on Real Estate and Personal Property, 1872, 1878, 1880–81, 1883–90
Circuit Court, Sumter County Courthouse, Livingston
August term, July 16–August 25, 1885
Final Record, 1887, XX
Minutes, April, 1880–February, 1885
National Archives Publications
Returns from Regular Army Infantry Regiments, June, 1821–December 1966, Microcopy 665, Roll 22
Rolls 169–73, reproducing file 2579–AGO 1874, in depth reports from Louisiana, Alabama, and South Carolina concerning the elections of 1874
Federal Records Center, East Point, Georgia
Assession No. 54A308 Record Group 21. This "packet" contains material relative to the Carnathan case.
Minutes, Circuit Court of the United States, December, 1880–October, 1884, Record Group 21 Book D

Miscellaneous
   Medical Records, State of Alabama, Department of
   Mental Health, Bryce Hospital, Tuscaloosa
   Ulmer, Isaac Barton, Papers, Southern Historical
   Collection, University of North Carolina, Chapel
   Hill

FEDERAL AND STATE DOCUMENTS

Acts of the General Assembly of Alabama, 1847–48,
   1849, 1859–60, 1874–75.
*Annual Report of the Secretary of War on the Operations
   of the Department,* I. Washington, D.C.: Government
   Printing Office, 1875.
*Biographical Directory of The American Congress, 1771–
   1961.* Washington, D.C.: Government Printing Office,
   1961.
Contested Election, James Gillette v. *Thomas H. Hern-
   don,* House Miscellaneous Document, 47th Congress,
   1st Session, V, No. 16.
Letford, William, compiler. *Alabama Congressional and
   Legislative Representation 1819 to 1960.* Montgomery: Walker Printing Co., [1960?].
Rowell, Chester H. *A Historical and Legal Digest of All
   the Contested Election Cases in the House of Representatives of the United States from the First to the
   Fifty-Sixth Congress, 1789–1901.* 56th Congress, 2nd
   Session, House Document No. 510.
United States Census Reports. Eighth (1860)–Tenth
   (1880).

NEWSPAPERS

Atlanta *Constitution,* 1882.
Birmingham *Iron Age,* 1882.
Bladon Springs *Herald,* 1872, 1874.
Butler *Choctaw County News,* 1876, 1878–81
Butler *Choctaw Herald,* 1874, 1884–85, 1887
Butler *Courier,* 1882–83.
Butler *News,* 1876–77.
Camden *News and Pacificator,* 1882.
Carrollton *West Alabamian,* 1882.
Charleston (South Carolina) *News and Courier,* 1882.
Chicago *Inter Ocean,* 1882.
Demopolis *Marengo News-Journal,* 1882.
Gainesville *Reporter,* 1882.
Greensboro *Alabama Beacon,* 1882.
Grove Hill *Clarke County Democrat,* 1882.
Hartford (Conn.) *Courant,* 1874, 1882.
Hayneville *Examiner,* 1882.
Huntsville *Gazette,* 1882.
Jackson (Miss.) *Weekly Clarion,* 1882.
Jacksonville *Republican,* 1882.
Linden *Reporter,* 1882.
Little Rock *Daily Arkansas Gazette,* 1882.
Livingston *Journal,* 1874, 1882–83.
Louisville (Ky.) *Courier-Journal,* 1882.
Macon (Ga.) *Telegram and Messenger,* 1882.
Marion *Commonwealth,* 1882.
Mobile *Daily Register,* 1880, 1882.
Montgomery *Advertiser,* 1874, 1876, 1882.
Montgomery *Alabama State Journal,* 1874.
Nashville (Tenn.) *Daily American,* 1882.

New Orleans *Daily Picayune,* 1882.
New Orleans *Times-Democrat,* 1882.
New York *Times,* 1882.
New York *Tribune,* 1882.
Opelika *Times,* 1882.
Pensacola (Fla.) *Semi-Weekly Commercial,* 1882.
Raleigh (N.C.) *News and Observer,* 1882.
Six Mile *Bibb Blade,* 1882.
Talladega *Our Mountain Home,* 1882.
Troy *Enquirer,* 1882.
Tuskaloosa *Gazette,* 1882.
Uniontown *Press,* 1882.
Washington (D.C.) *Post,* 1882.

BOOKS

Abernethy, Thomas Perkins. *The Formative Period in Alabama, 1815–1828.* University, Alabama: University of Alabama Press, 1965.

Ball, Rev. T. H. *A Glance Into The Great South-East, or Clarke County, Alabama, and Its Surroundings, from 1540 to 1877.* Grove Hill, Ala.: 1882.

Berney, Saffold. *Hand-Book of Alabama.* Birmingham: Roberts & Son, 1892.

De Rosier, Arthur H. *The Removal of the Choctaw Indians.* Knoxville: University of Tennessee Press, 1970.

De Santis, Vincent P. *Republicans Face the Southern Question: The New Departure Years, 1877–1897.* Baltimore: Johns Hopkins University Press, 1959.

Garrett, William. *Reminiscences of Public Men in Alabama for Thirty Years.* Atlanta: Plantation Publishing Company Press, 1872.

Fleming, Walter L. *Civil War and Reconstruction in*

Alabama. New York: Columbia University Press, 1905.

Going, Allen Johnston. *Bourbon Democracy in Alabama 1874–1890.* University, Ala.: University of Alabama Press, 1951.

Hirshon, Stanley P. *Farewell to the Bloody Shirt: Northern Republicans and the Southern Negro, 1877–1893.* Bloomington: Indiana University Press, 1962.

Massey, John. *Reminiscences Giving Sketches of Scenes Through Which the Author Has Passed and Pen Portraits of People Who Have Modified His Life.* Nashville: Publishing House of Methodist Episcopal Church, South, 1916.

McMilan, Malcolm Cook. *Constitutional Development in Alabama, 1798–1901: A Study in Politics, the Negro, and Sectionalism.* Chapel Hill: University of North Carolina Press, 1955.

Owen, Thomas McAdory. *History of Alabama and Dictionary of Alabama Biography.* 4 vols. Chicago: S. J. Clarke Publishing Company, 1921.

Sefton, James E. *The United States Army and Reconstruction 1865–1877.* Baton Rouge: Louisiana State University Press, 1967.

Tindall, George Brown. *South Carolina Negroes 1877–1900.* University of South Carolina Press, 1952.

Woodward, C. Vann. *Reunion and Reaction: The Compromise of 1877 and the End of Reconstruction.* Boston: Little, Brown, 1951.

ARTICLES

De Santis, Vincent. "President Arthur and the Independent Movement in the South in 1882," *Journal of Southern History,* XIX (August, 1953), 346–63.

————. "President Garfield and the Solid South," *North Carolina Historical Review,* XXVI (October, 1959), 442–65.

DuBose, Euba Eugenia. "The History of Mount Sterling," *Alabama Historical Quarterly,* XXV (Fall and Winter, 1963), 297–369. This study was originally a master's thesis completed at the University of Alabama in 1931.

Sloan, John Z. "The Ku Klux Klan and the Alabama Election of 1872," *Alabama Review,* XVIII (April, 1965), 113–23.

Roberts, Frances. "William Manning Lowe and the Greenback Party in Alabama," *Alabama Review,* V (April, 1952), 100–21.

Trelease, Allen W. "Who Were the Scalawags," *Journal of Southern History,* XXIX (November, 1963), 445–68.

Williamson, Edward C. "The Alabama Election of 1874," *Alabama Review,* XVII (July, 1964), 210–18.

Woolfolk, Sarah Van V. "Five Men Called Scalawags," *Alabama Review,* XVII (January, 1964), 45–55.

Index